GINO'S AIR FRYER COOKBOOK

GINO'S AIR FRYER COOKBOOK

Italian Classics Made Easy

PHOTOGRAPHY BY HAARALA HAMILTON

BLOOMSBURY PUBLISHING
LONDON · OXFORD · NEW YORK · NEW DELHI · SYDNEY

I think of my Mamma, Alba, whenever I use an air fryer.
She would have loved one!

CONTENTS

8   *Introduction*

14   Classic Italian

54   Ready in 20

82   Family

126   The Med Diet

146   Date Night

168   Sweet

200   *Index*

INTRODUCTION

I thought about buying an air fryer for a long time before I actually did, in fact for around a decade. I kept hearing so many good things about them, but I must admit it took a while for me to convince myself, mostly because I'd never really got my head around them. I just had a lot of questions going round in my mind. What are air fryers? Are they necessary? Or are they just another kitchen gadget that will gather dust in the cupboard?

Then, one day, I finally bought one. I figured that I couldn't be against air fryers without at least trying them, though I was sure I'd give mine away after a week or two.

Since then, I've bought myself another two and I am converted. I just love them. They're simple to use, efficient and environmentally friendly. In my opinion, air fryers are a must-have: they make your life easier in the kitchen while still enabling you to create fantastic food for your friends and family. The best thing of all is that Italian food cooks beautifully in an air fryer, which means a very happy Gino!

You can buy air fryers anywhere these days, even my local butcher sells them. When they first hit the shops, they were marketed as the perfect, healthier way to get the same results as deep-frying, but, these days, we know they can do so much more than that.

An air fryer works like a small fan oven, with temperatures ranging up to about 240°C, depending on the model you choose. Hot air circulates really fast around the air fryer basket and you need to use very little oil on the food, which makes it the ideal way to cook any dishes and ingredients that require dry heat. They're great at cooking burgers, chicken, steaks and sausages, of course, but they also give particularly good results for salmon and cod, or sardines and anchovies, or even shellfish such as prawns or scallops. Air fryers are perfect at cooking vegetables, too, such as courgettes, fennel, potatoes, aubergines or pumpkin. Pretty much everything goes in there. I love them so much, I've even designed and produced my own brand of air fryers!

Before you start cooking in an air fryer, there are a few things you need to know to get the best out of it, so turn the page for what I have learned.

SMOKING HOT: CHOOSING THE BEST OIL

When cooking with an air fryer, it's important to understand which oil to use. Oil heated to a high temperature will reach a 'smoking point', which both creates a burning smell and can be bad for you. So it's really important to use the correct oil for a recipe. To help you choose, my chart below approximates the different smoking points of various cooking oils (these can vary depending on how fresh the oil is, among other factors). Once you have read an air fryer recipe and know what temperature you will be cooking at, you will be able to select which of these oils will work best for that dish. (These numbers, apart from for extra virgin olive oil, are all for refined oils, rather than unrefined oils which will usually reach smoking point at a lower temperature.)

TYPE OF OIL	SMOKING POINT
Avocado oil	270°C
Corn oil	230°C
Peanut oil	230°C
Sunflower oil	230°C
Olive oil	220°C
Vegetable oil	220°C
Coconut oil	180°C
Extra virgin olive oil	170°C

In many air fryer recipes, it's suggested that you should cook with spray oil, which is great when you want to create a crispy coating without using lots of fat. In fact, an air fryer uses about 80 per cent less oil compared to deep-frying, so not only is it healthier, but much cheaper too. I must, however, be honest with you all: an air fryer will never take the place of a deep fryer, as some dishes and ingredients are cooked perfectly only when deep-fried. However, it's still an amazing alternative to shallow frying, or switching on a conventional oven.

GINO'S AIR FRYER HACKS

Now, before we start cooking, let me give you my top tips:

▶ In the past two years, as I've been working on this book, I have used a three-litre, a five-litre, a six-litre and occasionally a seven-litre air fryer. But all the recipes I've created for this book can easily be scaled up or down, depending on the size of your air fryer, so please do not panic: I've got your back. Air fryers come in a fantastic world of shapes and sizes, so where dimensions matter – which is only in a handful of these recipes – I've indicated the size of baking dish you should use, if your machine is larger.

▶ Always preheat your air fryer before putting in any food. It will only take a couple of minutes to preheat, but will make a huge difference to your dish... trust me.

▶ Do not overfill the air fryer. Instead, leave space between the ingredients to allow hot air to circulate around the food. If some recipes require the overlapping of ingredients, move them around more often during the cooking time and check on them: maybe they will sometimes require a little more time to cook to perfection.

▶ I've learned that any container that can be put into a regular oven can definitely go into an air fryer, so you have nothing to worry about on that front. Ovenproof ceramic, glass and terracotta, silicone and Pyrex are all perfectly fine to use. You can also use baking paper and cooking foil just as you would in a conventional oven.

▶ All three air fryers I've owned have the same great thing in common: they are super-super-easy to clean. So every time you've finished cooking, cool down the air fryer and ALWAYS clean it with soap and hot water as you would with your pots and pans. Do not leave any food residue in the air fryer, just as you wouldn't in a pan, as it will have harmful effects when you are cooking the next dish. Some air fryers are also dishwasher-proof, so no excuses please.

I have to dedicate this chapter to my Italian family, because every single recipe was either taught to me, or at least fed to me, by my mum, my two Nonnas, or – my inspiration and the man who I hope I've made proud – my grandpa and co-chef, Nonno Giovanni. All these dishes are my heritage and I have in turn passed them down to my children. They are also classics, of course, because they are among the most famous and popular Italian recipes.

I must admit, when I started writing this book, I was worried about this chapter, as there is a traditional way to make Italian dishes and it doesn't involve an air fryer. But I still found the process of cooking satisfying and didn't feel like too much of a cheat! As usual, I use only the freshest seasonal ingredients and try to stick to authentic methods as much as I can. For instance, in the aubergine Parmigiana recipe here, other than not salting the aubergines at the start, all the steps I take are almost identical to the classic way of assembling it. Using an air fryer to cook it, though, reduces both cooking time and washing-up... win-win! I'm sure Mamma would have approved.

The favourite recipe here among the girls in my life is *gnocchi alla Sorrentina*. My daughter Mia loves not only making this dish but wants to eat it at least once a week, whereas my boys will always ask for the tagliata topside. I think my personal favourite has to be the arancine. Not only do they remind me of my childhood – when I would eat them after school for a snack, or have them for a lunch on the go – but the air fryer really does get them so lovely and crispy and you can be as creative as you like with the fillings. In the past, I've used Bolognese sauce, cheese and truffle, ham and cheese, even leftover vegetables. They are so filling and tasty, perfect for canapés, starters or main courses and can be eaten hot or at room temperature. So whatever else you do, definitely give that recipe a try.

CLASSIC
ITALIAN

CANNELLONI WITH SPINACH AND RICOTTA

Cannelloni ricotta e spinaci

SERVES 4

For the sauce
1 tablespoon olive oil
1 garlic clove, finely sliced
700g tomato passata
1 teaspoon chopped
   thyme leaves
40g finely grated pecorino
   Romano cheese, plus more
   for the top
Salt and freshly ground
   black pepper

For the cannelloni
750g frozen spinach, defrosted
750g ricotta cheese, very
   well drained
½ small nutmeg, freshly grated
2 teaspoons chopped
   thyme leaves
12 fresh lasagne sheets, each
   about 16 × 11cm
20g salted butter, cut into
   small cubes

A perfect Sunday dish to enjoy with the family: comforting, filling and just delicious. It is a bit fiddly, but the result is worth every minute of your time, and, if your family is like mine where the kids aren't even up before noon at the weekend, put some music on and enjoy the moment! You can substitute the pecorino Romano for Parmesan cheese if you prefer. Please make sure you drain the ricotta well, or the filling will be too wet.

To make the sauce, heat the olive oil and garlic in a saucepan and fry over a medium-low heat for 30–60 seconds, stirring all the time with a wooden spoon. Pour in the passata and 100ml water, then season with the thyme, ½ teaspoon salt and ¼ teaspoon pepper. Increase the heat to medium-high and bring to a simmer, stirring constantly, for 2 minutes. Leave to simmer over a medium heat for 10 minutes, stirring occasionally. Turn off the heat, then stir in half the pecorino.

Meanwhile, squeeze all the excess water out of the spinach, then place in a bowl with the ricotta, the remaining 20g of pecorino, the nutmeg, thyme, ½ teaspoon salt and ¼ teaspoon pepper. Mix well with a wooden spoon.

Lay the lasagne sheets in front of you, with a shorter side facing you. Working quickly so the pasta doesn't dry out, brush them all with cold water. Divide the spinach mixture evenly between the lasagne sheets, spooning a portion in a line towards the base of each sheet, but leaving a 1cm border closest to you. Roll them up, neatening as you go and spreading the filling to evenly fill the tubes. Slice each into 3 smaller sausage shapes.

Preheat the air fryer to 150°C for 3 minutes.

Arrange the cannelloni in a 21cm square oven dish, or directly in the air fryer drawer if yours is the same size, brush again with water, then spoon over all the sauce. Cook for 25 minutes.

Increase the temperature to 160°C. Sprinkle over some pecorino and dot the cubed butter on top, grind over some pepper and cook for a further 15 minutes until golden and cooked through. Serve immediately.

SICILIAN AUBERGINES WITH RED WINE VINEGAR AND GREEN OLIVES

Caponata alla Siciliana

SERVES 4

400g aubergines (about
  2 small)
2 tablespoons olive oil
1 small shallot, roughly
  chopped into 3cm chunks
2 celery sticks, cut into
  2cm chunks
400g can of chopped
  tomatoes
1 tablespoon tomato purée
50g pitted green olives,
  roughly chopped
1 tablespoon capers in
  vinegar, drained
1 tablespoon light brown
  sugar, or to taste
30ml red wine vinegar, or
  to taste
1 tablespoon chopped
  mint leaves
1 tablespoon extra virgin
  olive oil
30g toasted pine nuts
Salt and freshly ground
  black pepper

I discovered this recipe when I was filming my Italian cooking show in Sicily and it really is super-tasty. If you don't like aubergines, please try it with courgettes or peppers instead, as they work equally well. This is fantastic to serve with fish or meat, or even try them in a panino with some Parma ham. You can substitute the green olives with Taggiasca pitted olives, if you prefer.

Preheat the air fryer to 180°C for 3 minutes.

Peel strips of skin off the aubergines, so they are striped black and white, then cut them into 4cm chunks. Toss the cubes with the regular olive oil and ½ teaspoon salt and cook in the air fryer fitted with the basket insert for 25 minutes, shaking to toss halfway, or until golden and cooked through. Set aside.

Tip the shallot, celery, chopped tomatoes, tomato purée, olives and capers into the air fryer drawer, mix with ¼ teaspoon salt, ¼ teaspoon pepper and 50ml water, then cook for 15 minutes.

Tip the roast aubergine into the tomato sauce, add the sugar and vinegar and mix well with a wooden spoon. Cook for a further 10 minutes.

Stir in the mint, taste and adjust the vinegar, sugar and seasoning. Spoon into a serving dish, drizzle over the extra virgin olive oil, then top with the pine nuts when ready to serve.

COURGETTE AND FONTINA TART WITH SEMI-DRIED TOMATOES

Torta salata con fontina e pomodorini semi-secchi

SERVES 4

1 large aubergine, about 300g
320g sheet of puff pastry
1 large courgette, about 350g, cut into slices
2 teaspoons olive oil
2 eggs
150g fontina cheese, cut into 5mm slices
50g semi-dried tomatoes, halved if large
2 tablespoons fine semolina or polenta
Salt and freshly ground black pepper

This is definitely my kind of food and is absolutely perfect for vegetarians, or equally fantastic with a platter of Italian ham and salami. Add a large yellow pepper if you fancy: just cut it into chunks and roast in the air fryer along with the courgette and aubergine. Substitute the fontina cheese with a good-quality Cheddar if you prefer, or goat's cheese also works well.

Preheat the air fryer to 180°C for 3 minutes.

Peel strips of skin off the aubergine, so it is striped black and white, then cut it into 3cm chunks.

Unroll the pastry, cut out a circle, then freeze for 10 minutes, to firm up.

Meanwhile, place the courgette slices and aubergine chunks in the air fryer fitted with the basket insert, toss with the oil, ½ teaspoon salt and ¼ teaspoon pepper. Cook for 5 minutes, shake to toss, then cook for a further 5 minutes.

Break 1 egg into a bowl and lightly beat. Tip the cooked vegetables into the bowl, add the cheese and tomatoes and mix well.

Take the pastry out of the freezer and lay on a flat surface. Sprinkle the semolina in the centre, covering about the size of your hand. Spoon the vegetables on top in an even layer, leaving a 4cm border. Reduce the air fryer temperature to 160°C.

Lightly beat the second egg in a small bowl. Using a pastry brush, brush the pastry border all over with some of the beaten egg.

Fold all the sides over the vegetables towards the middle, leaving a circle of vegetables showing. Brush the folded-over pastry with the remaining egg, then set the tart directly in the air fryer fitted with the basket insert.

Cook for 1 hour, covering with foil halfway through so it does not scorch, then lift out and serve.

BOLOGNESE-STYLE SAUCE

Ragù stile Bolognese

SERVES 6

20g salted butter
2 tablespoons olive oil
100g pancetta lardons
1 bay leaf
1 onion, finely chopped
1 large carrot, finely chopped
1 celery stick, finely chopped
300g minced beef
300g minced pork
250ml Italian red wine
175ml chicken stock, or
   beef stock
400g tomato passata
75ml whole milk
Salt and freshly ground
   black pepper

An absolutely essential recipe that every Italian is taught. I like to add milk, which both lightens the sauce and helps tenderise the meat. The concentrated heat of an air fryer gives the sauce a delicious deep flavour, which is fantastic. You can substitute the minced pork with minced lamb if you fancy a change, and please use a reasonable quality wine: if it's not good enough to drink, it's not good enough for cooking.

Heat the butter, 1 tablespoon of the oil and the pancetta in a saucepan over a medium heat and cook for 2 minutes. Add the bay leaf, onion, carrot and celery, mix well with a wooden spoon and cook for a further 8 minutes until the vegetables are soft, stirring regularly.

Preheat the air fryer to 180°C for 3 minutes.

Meanwhile, put the remaining 1 tablespoon oil into the air fryer drawer along with both the minced meats and mix with your hands to roughly combine. Cook for 8 minutes to brown. Use a wooden spoon to turn the minced meat; it will have shrunk into chunks, but don't break them up just yet. Cook for a further 5 minutes.

Pour the wine into your vegetables and boil briskly for 2–3 minutes, until the liquid has reduced by two-thirds. Add the stock, passata, 1 teaspoon salt and ½ teaspoon pepper, return to the boil, then reduce the heat to a fast simmer for 8 minutes, stirring often with a wooden spoon. Reduce the heat to low, pour in the milk and cook for 1 minute, stirring constantly.

Reduce the air fryer temperature to 150°C.

Take the air fryer drawer out, set it on a work surface and break up the minced meat with a wooden spoon. Tip the sauce into the air fryer and mix well. Cover with foil, then set a small ovenproof plate or a couple of forks on top of the foil to stop it blowing off; this will ensure the ragù is covered securely. Cook for 50 minutes. Taste and add more salt and pepper to your liking. Serve with any pasta of your choice, or use it in a Classic lasagne, or even in Roasted stuffed peppers with Bolognese sauce and mozzarella (see pages 24 and 79).

CLASSIC LASAGNE

Lasagne alla Bolognese

SERVES 4

For the béchamel

85g salted butter
70g plain flour
850ml chilled whole milk
40g finely grated Parmesan
  cheese
¼ small nutmeg, freshly grated
Salt and freshly ground
  black pepper

For the rest

8 fresh lasagne sheets, each
  about 16 × 11cm
1 quantity Bolognese-style
  sauce (see page 23)
30g finely grated Parmesan
  cheese
20g cold butter, cut into
  small cubes

A traditional Sunday dish served in many Italian households, now improved by the golden and deliciously crispy top you get in an air fryer. The secret is to let it rest for a good 15 minutes before serving, so it will hold together well. When cooking this in a regular oven, it doesn't matter what pasta you use, but if you use an air fryer, you need fresh lasagne sheets. You can substitute the Parmesan with pecorino Sardo or Grana Padano cheese, if you prefer.

To make the béchamel, melt the butter in a saucepan over a medium heat. Stir in the flour using a handheld whisk and cook for 1 minute until light brown in colour. Gradually whisk in the milk, then reduce the heat to low and cook for 8 minutes, gently whisking from time to time. Once thickened, stir in the 40g Parmesan, ½ teaspoon salt, ½ teaspoon pepper and the nutmeg. Set aside to cool slightly.

Preheat the air fryer to 150°C for 3 minutes.

Now it's time to layer the lasagne. You can do this in a 21cm square baking dish, or directly in the air fryer drawer, if yours is the same size.

Spread one-quarter of the béchamel in the dish or air fryer drawer. Lay 2 lasagne sheets on top; you'll need to trim one and add the trimmed piece to the gap above the sheets. Spread one-third of the Bolognese sauce over the pasta. Then repeat the process twice more to create layers, finishing with the last 2 pasta sheets and spreading the final one-quarter of the béchamel on top. Place in the air fryer and cook for 20 minutes.

Increase the air fryer temperature to 160°C.

Sprinkle over the 30g Parmesan and dot with the cubed butter. Finally, grind some pepper over and cook for a further 35 minutes until golden and cooked through. Let it rest for at least 15 minutes, then serve.

SLICED COURGETTES WITH MINT, GARLIC AND WHITE WINE VINEGAR

Zucchine alla scapece

SERVES 4

500g courgettes, sliced into
    5mm rounds
50ml extra virgin olive oil
20ml white wine vinegar
2 garlic cloves, finely sliced
15 mint leaves
Salt and freshly ground
    black pepper

I absolutely love this dish, as it reminds me of summer. When cooking these the traditional way, I spend a long time grilling each courgette slice on a griddle pan. That is fine when you are on holiday, but an air fryer saves so much time and they are just as delicious. The courgettes really cook down, so I would suggest air frying them in two batches, if you have a smaller air fryer. You can spice them up with fresh chillies and also add some Leccino black olives, if you fancy. Keep them refrigerated if you don't plan to eat them straight away.

Place the courgette slices in a colander, sprinkle with 1 tablespoon salt and toss to distribute. Cover with a tea towel and leave to drain excess liquid for 30 minutes. Lightly rinse the slices and gently squeeze them dry.

Preheat the air fryer to 170°C for 3 minutes.

Toss the sliced courgettes in the air fryer fitted with the basket insert in 1 tablespoon of the oil until evenly coated. The slices can overlap, but they shouldn't be stacked on top of each other. (You may need to cook these in 2 batches, depending on the size of your air fryer.) Cook for 18–20 minutes, shaking to toss again halfway through cooking.

In a bowl, mix the rest of the oil with some salt, pepper, the vinegar, garlic and mint. Add the courgettes while still warm, to soak up the dressing. Eat straight away, or they're even better if you leave them for a day to let the flavours develop.

GNOCCHI WITH TOMATO, MOZZARELLA AND BASIL

Gnocchi alla Sorrentina

SERVES 4

1 large garlic clove, crushed
400g tomato passata
2 tablespoons tomato purée
800g good-quality shop-bought potato gnocchi
10 basil leaves, chopped
200g buffalo mozzarella ball, torn
30g finely grated pecorino Romano cheese
Salt and freshly ground black pepper

The classic way to serve gnocchi in the town of Sorrento. My mother used to work in Sorrento and I remember, as a little boy, she would take me to work with her. At lunchtime, we would go to a little trattoria on the corner and order gnocchi alla Sorrentina. This is super-easy to make, so it's perfect for a quick midweek dinner. You can substitute the buffalo mozzarella with any other mozzarella ball, if you prefer.

Preheat the air fryer to 200°C for 3 minutes.

Put the garlic and passata in the air fryer drawer with the tomato purée, ½ teaspoon salt and ¼ teaspoon pepper. Mix well using a wooden spoon and cook for 12 minutes.

Meanwhile, in a large saucepan, bring 2 litres of water with 1 teaspoon salt to the boil. Cook the gnocchi according to the instructions on the packet: they will float to the surface when ready. Drain, then add to the sauce in the air fryer drawer with most of the basil (keeping a little back for serving). Mix well and cook for 12 minutes.

Reduce the air fryer temperature to 190°C.

Top the gnocchi evenly with the mozzarella, sprinkle over the pecorino cheese and cook for a further 8 minutes until golden. Sprinkle over the remaining basil and serve immediately.

SUCCULENT MEATBALLS WITH SPICY TOMATO SAUCE

Polpette con salsa all'arrabbiata

SERVES 4

70g crustless white bread
100ml whole milk
1 egg, lightly beaten
500g minced beef
300g minced pork
1 large garlic clove, crushed
2 tablespoons finely chopped
    flat leaf parsley leaves
60g finely grated pecorino
    Romano cheese
40g dried breadcrumbs
4 tablespoons olive oil
Salt and freshly ground
    black pepper

For the sauce

1 tablespoon olive oil
1 garlic clove, crushed
600g tomato passata
½ teaspoon chilli flakes,
    or chilli oil, or to taste
20 basil leaves

By far my daughter Mia's favourite dinner of all time. She loves both eating meatballs and making them! I serve these with boiled rice and chunks of warm bread to dunk up the sauce. You can make them with just minced beef, if you don't want to use pork.

Break the bread up into a large bowl and pour over the milk, then leave for 2 minutes. Using your fingertips, mix the bread and milk together to create a wet paste. Add the egg, minced beef and pork, garlic, parsley, pecorino, 1 teaspoon salt and ½ teaspoon pepper. Mix well with your hands, then roll into 12 meatballs.

Pour the dried breadcrumbs into a wide, shallow bowl. In a small bowl, toss the meatballs in the olive oil, using your hands to coat entirely, then place the meatballs in the breadcrumbs and roll around gently to lightly coat all over. Press the crumbs lightly into any missed patches.

Preheat the air fryer to 180°C for 3 minutes.

Place the meatballs in the air fryer fitted with the basket insert and cook for 20 minutes until browned and cooked through.

Meanwhile, prepare the sauce. Place the olive oil and garlic in a large shallow saucepan and fry over a medium heat for 30 seconds, stirring all the time with a wooden spoon. Pour in the passata and chilli flakes or oil, and stir, then add the basil, 1 teaspoon salt and ½ teaspoon pepper, bring to the boil and stir for 2 minutes. Reduce the heat slightly and leave to simmer for 15 minutes, stirring occasionally. Gently toss the meatballs in the sauce and serve immediately.

MILANESE-STYLE AIR FRYER RISOTTO WITH SAFFRON AND WINE

Risotto al forno stile Milanese

SERVES 4

½–1 teaspoon saffron threads, to taste
70g unsalted butter
1 onion, finely chopped
300g arborio rice, or carnaroli rice, or vialone nano rice
175ml dry white wine
1 small bay leaf
900ml vegetable stock, or chicken stock
75g finely grated Parmesan cheese, plus more to serve
Salt and freshly ground black pepper

With risotto cooked the regular way, you have to stand over a hob the whole time. In this recipe, though you still start it at the hob, you then have the freedom to walk away and do other things. A simply flavoured risotto, this is great on its own, or makes a fantastic side dish to fish, vegetables or meat. To make it extra-sexy, add chopped ham, peas or semi-dried tomatoes during the last 5 minutes of cooking.

In a small bowl, mix the saffron with 100ml warm water and set aside to infuse.

In a large saucepan, heat 30g of the butter over a low heat, add the onion and cook for 10 minutes, stirring occasionally with a wooden spoon, so the onion sweats down but doesn't brown. Add the rice, mix well to coat the grains in butter and cook for 1 minute. Pour in the wine, stir and cook for a further 1 minute, allowing the alcohol to evaporate.

Increase the heat to medium, add the bay leaf, stock, ½ teaspoon salt and ¼ teaspoon pepper. Bring to the boil, stirring occasionally with a wooden spoon. Once it's boiling, reduce the heat to a medium-fast simmer and let it bubble for 5 minutes.

Preheat the air fryer to 150°C for 3 minutes.

Tip the risotto into the air fryer drawer and cook for 20 minutes.

Stir in the remaining butter, the grated Parmesan cheese and saffron liquid. Reduce the air fryer temperature to 140°C and cook for a further 10–15 minutes for an al dente bite. Cook for 5–10 minutes longer if you prefer your rice softer, or if you're using the risotto to make arancine, such as Crispy arancine with ham and mozzarella (see overleaf).

Taste the risotto and adjust the salt and pepper, then serve immediately with Parmesan shavings.

CRISPY ARANCINE WITH HAM AND MOZZARELLA

Arancine con prosciutto cotto e mozzarella

MAKES 6

1 quantity Milanese-style air fryer risotto with saffron and wine (see page 33), made following the arancine timings and cooled completely

For the filling
60g cooked ham, chopped
60g mozzarella cucina, chopped into 6 even cubes
1 tablespoon finely grated pecorino Sardo

For the coating
100g panko breadcrumbs
1 tablespoon olive oil
1 large egg, lightly beaten
2 tablespoons olive oil

A classic Sicilian street food. These were originally made to eat on the go, and, in Italy, can be as big as a tennis ball. You can fill them with so many things, from chopped ham, to peas or fried courgettes, cheeses and truffle, or even Bolognese-style sauce (see page 23), so be as creative as you like. They are super-filling and perfect for a picnic or working lunch, as they can be eaten hot or at room temperature. They are even fantastic for a party canapé, with a cold glass of prosecco. A top tip: run your hands under cold water to help stop the rice sticking when you're shaping them.

In a small bowl, mix all the filling ingredients together using a metal spoon. Now loosen the rice with your hands in a separate bowl, squeezing and breaking down the grains as you go, for about 5 minutes. Divide the rice into 6 portions.

One at a time, flatten a rice portion in the palm of your hand, make a little well in the centre and put a heaped tablespoon of filling in there, including a cube of mozzarella in each. Mould the rice around the filling to seal it in, squeezing and pressing the rice to compress it, to ensure it holds its shape.

Place the breadcrumbs in a medium bowl, pour in the oil and mix using your fingertips as you would when making a crumble. Put the egg in a separate bowl.

One at a time, coat the arancine balls lightly in the breadcrumbs, rolling them gently so the whole surface is lightly covered. Dip in the beaten egg, let any excess drip off, then place back in the breadcrumbs, pressing them lightly into any missed patches. Place on a tray, cover lightly with clingfilm and refrigerate for 2 hours, or even overnight.

Preheat the air fryer to 170°C for 3 minutes.

Take the arancine balls straight from the fridge, gently place in the air fryer fitted with the basket insert and cook for 25 minutes. Leave to stand for 5 minutes, then serve.

POTATO CAKE

Gâteau di patate

SERVES 4

For the cake

800g potatoes, peeled and
  cut into 4cm chunks
40g dried breadcrumbs
2 egg yolks
110g cooked ham, sliced
125g mozzarella ball, torn
  into pieces
15g salted butter, cut into
  small cubes
Salt and freshly ground
  black pepper

For the béchamel

80g salted butter, plus more for
  the tin
60g plain flour
700ml chilled whole milk
75g finely grated Parmesan
  cheese, plus more for the top
¼ nutmeg, freshly grated

A traditional Neapolitan savoury cake. The simple name does not
do this recipe justice, as the flavours and textures create the perfect
comfort food. Traditionally, it was eaten at room temperature or
warm, with antipasti, but these days most Italians would have it
as supper, with a crisp salad to offset the richness. It is what we
Italians call *piatto unico*: a 'one-dish wonder'. My biggest tip is
to rest it for 10 minutes before serving, allowing it to settle and
making your life easier when portioning. If you prefer, substitute the
ham with mortadella, salami or Parma ham. Children love this.

Bring 1.8 litres of water to the boil with 1 teaspoon of salt. Once at a
rolling boil, add the potatoes and cook for 15 minutes until tender, then
drain and set aside in a colander to steam dry for 5 minutes.

Meanwhile, butter a 17cm square cake tin, then sprinkle with the
breadcrumbs, tilting the tin to help them get to all the edges. Tip out the
excess and reserve for the top.

To make the béchamel, melt the butter in a saucepan over a medium
heat. Stir in the flour using a whisk and cook for 1 minute until it becomes
light brown in colour. Gradually whisk in the milk, reduce the heat to low,
and cook for 8 minutes, whisking gently but constantly. Once thickened,
stir in the Parmesan, 1 teaspoon salt, ½ teaspoon pepper and the
nutmeg. Take off the heat and allow to cool for 5 minutes.

While still warm, mash the potatoes with 30g béchamel and ½ teaspoon
each of salt and pepper. Beat the egg yolks into the mash, mix until
smooth and creamy, taste and add more salt and pepper as you like.

Preheat the air fryer to 150°C for 3 minutes. Spread half the mash in
the prepared tin. Add the remaining béchamel, then dot the ham and
mozzarella on top. Spread the remaining mash on top, right to the edges.
Cook for 20 minutes.

Increase the air fryer temperature to 160°C and cook for 10 minutes
more, then dot the butter over with the reserved breadcrumbs and a little
Parmesan. Cook for 10 minutes more until golden. Allow to stand for
10 minutes before digging in: it will be oozy in the middle, but will firm up
the longer you leave it. This is great hot or at room temperature.

TOPSIDE TAGLIATA WITH ROCKET, PARMESAN AND BALSAMIC

Tagliata di manzo con rucola, scaglie di parmigiano e aceto balsamico

SERVES 8

1.7kg beef topside joint,
   removed from the fridge
   1 hour before cooking
2 teaspoons olive oil
20g salted butter, at room
   temperature, cut into
   small cubes
2 rosemary sprigs
100g rocket leaves
5 tablespoons balsamic glaze
60g Parmesan shavings
½ teaspoon sea salt flakes
Salt and freshly ground
   black pepper

In Italy, we make tagliata with sirloin steak, but a thicker piece of meat cooks better in an air fryer, as it can get browned all over without becoming overcooked in the centre. This is perfect for a Sunday roast with a difference. You can substitute the Parmesan cheese with a good-quality mature Cheddar, if you prefer.

Preheat the air fryer to 210°C for 3 minutes.

Dry the beef with kitchen paper, then rub with the olive oil, 1 teaspoon salt and ½ teaspoon pepper. Press the butter cubes on top and rub to spread them all over.

Put the beef in the air fryer drawer and top with the rosemary sprigs. Cook for 25 minutes.

Reduce the air fryer temperature to 150°C. Continue to cook the beef for a further 5–10 minutes for rare meat, 15–20 minutes for medium, or 25–30 minutes for well done. (If your topside is a thinner piece, it may need a few minutes less.)

Place the beef on a carving board, cover with foil to keep warm and rest for 10 minutes.

Arrange the rocket leaves on a large serving platter. Slice the beef into 1cm-thick slices and lay on top of the rocket. Drizzle over the balsamic glaze and scatter the Parmesan shavings on top.

Sprinkle over the sea salt flakes and serve immediately.

AUBERGINE PARMIGIANA WITH SPICED TOMATO AND OOZING MOZZARELLA

Melanzane alla Parmigiana

SERVES 4

2 large aubergines
4–5 tablespoons olive oil
250g grated mozzarella
    cheese
60g finely grated Parmesan
    cheese

For the sauce
1 tablespoon olive oil
1 garlic clove, crushed
500g tomato passata
1–2 tablespoons chilli oil,
    or to taste
20 basil leaves
50g mascarpone
Salt and freshly ground
    black pepper

No one can make *melanzane alla Parmigiana* like my mum could, not even me, but this – her slightly adapted recipe – comes close. I'll be honest, this dish is still a labour of love even in an air fryer, but you don't need to salt the aubergines as you do in the traditional recipe, as they won't soak up oil the way they do in a frying pan, so that saves a step. If there is any left over, eat it at room temperature next day in a crispy ciabatta: a must-try.

Trim and peel the aubergines, then slice lengthways into 5mm-thick slices. Preheat the air fryer to 200°C for 3 minutes.

Rub or brush the olive oil lightly over the aubergine slices, then set on a tray or plate. It will take about 3 batches to cook them all. Place your first batch in the air fryer fitted with the basket insert so they're only overlapping a little and cook for 8 minutes. Remove and repeat the process until all the slices have been cooked.

Meanwhile, prepare the sauce. Place the olive oil and the garlic in a large shallow saucepan and fry over a medium heat for 30–60 seconds, stirring all the time with a wooden spoon. Pour in the passata, chilli oil, basil, 1½ teaspoons salt and 1 teaspoon pepper and stir for 2 minutes.

Add the mascarpone, stir to combine, then reduce the heat slightly and leave to simmer for 12 minutes. Taste: this is the time to add a bit more chilli oil if you want a stronger kick. Set aside.

Reduce the air fryer temperature to 180°C.

Lay one-third of the aubergine in a deep oven dish that fits in the air fryer (mine measured 20 × 20 × 6cm), or directly into the air fryer drawer, if yours is the same size, ideally lined with a silicone liner. Ladle over just under one-quarter of the sauce. Sprinkle over 60g mozzarella and 20g Parmesan. Repeat the layers twice more. You'll have extra sauce and mozzarella left to make a last layer; this is absorbed through the dish while it cooks and helps keep it extra-moist. Sprinkle over a pinch of pepper and air fry for 10 minutes.

Reduce the air fryer temperature to 160°C and bake for 20 minutes or until hot right through and browned on top. Leave to rest for 15 minutes, then serve.

ROMAN-STYLE GNOCCHI WITH PECORINO ROMANO

Gnocchi alla Romana

SERVES 4

700ml whole milk
1 bay leaf
165g semolina, ideally fine
   semolina
65g salted butter, cut into
   small cubes
100g finely grated pecorino
   Romano cheese
Freshly grated nutmeg
2 egg yolks
Salt and freshly ground
   black pepper

Bored with roast potatoes? Try this instead. Semolina is one of those ingredients that is often passed over, yet it can create some amazing dishes, this recipe included. These gnocchi are so tasty. I love them alongside a meat main course, but also they are absolutely delicious just with tomato sauce (see page 16). You can add finely chopped cooked ham to the semolina mixture for a different flavour, if you fancy.

Heat the milk and bay leaf in a large saucepan over a medium heat until very hot, but not boiling. Add the semolina gradually in a steady stream, whisking constantly. Once all the semolina is added and the mixture is thickening, beat with a wooden spoon for 1 minute.

Reduce the heat to low and keep beating for about 5 minutes: the mix will come away from the sides of the saucepan and become paste-like in texture. Mix in half the butter and half the cheese, some nutmeg, ½ teaspoon salt and ½ teaspoon pepper.

Take off the heat, then mix in the egg yolks, one at a time. Scrape the mixture, while still hot, on to a baking tray lined with baking paper, using a rubber spatula to spread it out to a thickness of 2cm. Level the top and leave to cool completely (it will take about 20 minutes).

Preheat the air fryer to 170°C for 3 minutes.

Using a 5cm diameter pastry cutter, cut out as many discs as you can and layer them in an oven dish that will fit in the air fryer, so they overlap slightly. Use your hands to reshape the offcuts and cut more discs, layering them into the dish as well. Sprinkle over the rest of the cheese and dot with the remaining butter.

Cook for 15–20 minutes until golden.

ITALIAN MEATLOAF WITH PARMA HAM AND PROVOLONE CHEESE

Polpettone classico con prosciutto crudo e formaggio

SERVES 4–6

50g crustless white bread
90ml whole milk
250g minced pork
250g minced beef
1 tablespoon finely chopped
   flat leaf parsley leaves
30g finely grated Parmesan
   cheese
1 teaspoon freshly grated
   nutmeg
1 egg
2 pinches of freshly ground
   white pepper
6 slices of Parma ham
150g provolone cheese, sliced
2 teaspoons extra virgin
   olive oil
Salt and freshly ground
   black pepper

Just like my Nonna Flora used to make. I'm not sure whether she would be mortified or thrilled at her recipe being cooked in an air fryer, but I'm guessing as long as it tasted the same, she would give us a thumbs-up of approval. I can honestly say that I can't tell the difference, that's the beauty of air fryers. The cheese and the milk help the meatloaf keep super-moist, yet the fryer gets it nice and golden outside. You can substitute the minced pork with minced lamb, and the provolone cheese with Taleggio or a good mature Cheddar if you prefer. This goes perfectly with my Roasted peppers with parsley, garlic and extra virgin olive oil (see overleaf).

Break the bread up into a large bowl and pour over the milk, then leave for 2 minutes. Using your fingertips, mix the bread and milk together to create a wet paste. Add the minced meats and combine. Now add the parsley, Parmesan and nutmeg, crack in the egg and season generously with salt and both the white and black peppers. Using your hand, mix all the ingredients together.

Set a large sheet of clingfilm on a work surface and place the meat mixture on top. Flatten it to make a 1cm-thick rectangle, measuring about 23 × 18cm. Place the Parma ham slices in an even layer on top of the meat, then the Provolone cheese slices on top of the ham.

Roll it up from a shorter side, using the clingfilm to help you keep it together. Seal the edge, then press the meatloaf together along its length to make it shorter but more compacted. Now wrap the roll in the clingfilm and let it rest in the fridge for 30 minutes.

Preheat the air fryer to 180°C for 3 minutes, with a silicone liner or a sheet of baking paper inside.

Remove the clingfilm from the meatloaf. Brush with the oil, place in the air fryer fitted with the basket insert and cook for 35–40 minutes, until browned and cooked through. Serve with salad or seasonal vegetables.

ROASTED PEPPERS WITH PARSLEY, GARLIC AND EXTRA VIRGIN OLIVE OIL

Peperoni arrostiti

SERVES 4

3 large peppers, total weight
   about 600g
20ml extra virgin olive oil
2 teaspoons finely chopped
   flat leaf parsley leaves
2 tablespoons red wine
   vinegar
1 garlic clove, crushed
Salt and freshly ground
   black pepper

These are just so tasty. They work with any meat or fish dish, or if you simply add feta, mozzarella or goat's cheese, you have created a delicious salad or sandwich filling. The bigger the peppers the better here, as they will be easier to peel, and please try to use a really good-quality extra virgin olive oil, as you will taste the difference. You can substitute the parsley with mint leaves, if you prefer. Only use red or yellow peppers, as they are sweeter.

Preheat the air fryer to 200°C for 3 minutes.

Line the air fryer basket insert with baking paper. Rub the peppers all over with 1 teaspoon extra virgin olive oil, then place them in the air fryer fitted with the lined basket insert. Cook the peppers for 25 minutes, shaking to toss halfway.

Once cooked, set the peppers aside to cool in the paper. Remove the skin from the peppers by peeling it off with your hands: it will come away easily. Remove the seeds, then tear into fillets.

Place the parsley, vinegar, garlic, ¼ teaspoon salt, ¼ teaspoon pepper and the remaining oil in a small, shallow bowl and add the pepper fillets. Toss gently, ensuring all the peppers are coated. Serve immediately with any meat or fish dish, or refrigerate for later.

CRISPY-CRACKLING PORK LOIN IN MILK AND SAGE

Arrosto di maiale con latte e salvia

SERVES 6

1.25kg boneless rolled pork loin joint with crackling, scored, removed from the fridge 1 hour before cooking
1 tablespoon olive oil
2 tablespoons sea salt flakes
600ml whole milk
3 garlic cloves, whole but roughly bashed
1 bay leaf
3 sage sprigs
Juice of ½ lemon and 2 broad strips of its zest, removed with a vegetable peeler
½ teaspoon freshly grated nutmeg
1 tablespoon finely chopped flat leaf parsley leaves
2 teaspoons finely chopped chives
Salt and freshly ground black pepper

Getting bored with traditional Sunday roasts? Try this super-easy recipe for a change and serve it with all your usual trimmings. The milk makes the meat deliciously tender; it will appear as though it has slightly curdled, but don't worry, that's how it's supposed to look after cooking. You can also replace the pork with a nice beef loin, just shorten the cooking time to match the way you like your beef cooked (see page 39). Substitute the sage with rosemary, too, if you prefer the flavour.

Preheat the air fryer to 200°C for 3 minutes.

Dry the pork skin with kitchen paper, then rub it all over with the oil and sea salt flakes. Place in the air fryer drawer skin side up and cook for 25 minutes.

Pour the milk in at the side (not over the meat) and add the garlic, bay leaf, sage, zest strips, nutmeg, ½ teaspoon salt and ½ teaspoon pepper.

Reduce the air fryer temperature to 160°C and cook for 1 hour 10 minutes. Remove the pork, cover with foil and let rest for a couple of minutes.

Meanwhile, season the milk with the lemon juice and a generous pinch of salt and pepper to taste, then stir in the parsley and chives. Carve the meat and serve it with the cooking juices poured over.

CHICKEN SALTIMBOCCA WITH PARMA HAM, SAGE AND MARSALA

Saltimbocca alla Romana

SERVES 4

4 skinless chicken breasts,
    about 180g each
8 slices of Parma ham
16 small sage leaves
30g salted butter, cubed
100ml Marsala wine
1 lemon
Salt and freshly ground
    black pepper

This traditional Roman dish is very much loved by all in the D'Acampo family, but most of all by my wife. If ever I'm in the dog house – and I must say that's not very often – this is the recipe I will make and serve her, it's her absolute favourite meal of all time. The salty Parma ham and sweet flavour of the Marsala wine are a match made in heaven and a must-try. You can substitute the Marsala with any sweet dessert wine you like.

Place the chicken breasts on a chopping board, cover with clingfilm and use a meat mallet or rolling pin to gently tap out each breast until flattened. Cut the breasts in half widthways to give you 8 pieces in total. (You can get your butcher to do this for you, if you prefer.)

Season each chicken piece with a little pinch of salt and pepper and lay on a slice of Parma ham. Top each with 2 sage leaves, then secure the ham and sage leaves to the chicken with a cocktail stick, threading it through the layers and keeping them as flat as possible.

Preheat the air fryer to 190°C for 3 minutes.

Place the saltimbocca directly in the air fryer drawer, sage side up, add the butter cubes on top and cook for 2 minutes. Pour in the Marsala wine and a squeeze of lemon juice and cook for a further 6 minutes until cooked through. Remove the cocktail sticks and serve on warmed plates with the juices. This is great with a dish of Sliced courgettes with mint, garlic and white wine vinegar alongside (see page 26).

All the recipes here literally take 20 minutes or less to cook, and more than half of them are ready from start to finish in 20 minutes, too. Having three children, life is busy and sometimes we just need to feed the family quickly, but we still want to give them something nutritious and wholesome after long days at school or work, or hours spent running around a cold sports field. My honey-glazed cod, pizza chicken and pork in crispy breadcrumbs are perfect for those occasions. Of course, on those odd few nights when you really can't be bothered, a takeaway is always nice, but quite often you can create a better, healthier and cheaper meal at home. And, of course, using the air fryer to do so makes life that much easier.

My pizza puff sticks are fun to make and perfect to serve at a dinner party as a canapé or a starter with a soup, leaving you more time to spend with your guests, while my courgette fries work with any main meal and are a must-try. Another D'Acampo favourite is the stuffed peppers, which are so easy if you have some Bolognese sauce stashed in the freezer. They look great, taste amazing and can be prepared in the morning or even a day before, so all you have to do when you get home is pop them in the air fryer. Now that's what I call fast food!

I make, serve and eat the recipes in this chapter all the time, as I depend on them to get us all through the week deliciously. So for those of you who are cooking for busy families and have hectic lives, I hope they help a little.

READY
IN 20

GARLIC BREAD WITH PARSLEY AND SMOKED PAPRIKA

Pane all'aglio, prezzemolo e paprika

SERVES 4–6

150g salted butter, very soft
3 large or 4 small garlic
  cloves, crushed
½ teaspoon sweet smoked
  paprika, plus more to sprinkle
3 tablespoons finely chopped
  flat leaf parsley leaves
1 ciabatta loaf, about 250g
Sea salt flakes

So very simple. I love this recipe because, honestly, anything goes. I've substituted the parsley with chives or rosemary, I've added Parmesan cheese or finely chopped black olives, and I've even mixed chocolate-hazelnut spread such as Nutella with the butter instead of garlic, herbs and spices, and all variations are amazing. A great tip is to quadruple the amounts for the garlic butter and freeze three portions separately for the next few times you make it.

In a small bowl, mix the butter with a wooden spoon for about 2 minutes, to lighten and loosen. Add the garlic, paprika, parsley and 1 teaspoon sea salt flakes. Mix until well combined.

Carefully cut 10 evenly spaced, deep slits into the ciabatta, ensuring you don't go all the way through, so the bread stays in a single piece. Spread the garlic butter into the gaps as evenly as you can. Sprinkle over some more sea salt flakes and another pinch of paprika.

Preheat the air fryer to 190°C for 3 minutes.

You may have to cut the loaf in half, depending on the size of your air fryer. Wrap the ciabatta in foil and cook for 10 minutes. Open the foil, then cook for a further 10 minutes. Serve with anything, but this is perfect with minestrone soup!

BAKED RICOTTA AND COURGETTES WITH ROSEMARY AND PISTACHIO NUTS

Ricotta e zucchine con rosmarino e pistacchi

SERVES 2

250g ricotta
2 tablespoons olive oil
1 rosemary sprig
1 large courgette (about
    250g), cut into 5cm fingers
20g pistachio nuts, roughly
    chopped
Salt and freshly ground
    black pepper
Focaccia or ciabatta, to serve

A fantastic super-quick meal, or antipasti option to share. I think we always feel we have to make a 'proper' dinner consisting of meat or fish, veg and a carb, when actually, this is so simple and quick, has so much flavour and is so super-filling that there really is no need for anything else. For an extra flavour, you can drizzle some maple syrup or honey over the ricotta before cooking. Try it: you won't be disappointed.

Preheat the air fryer to 190°C for 3 minutes.

Drain any liquid from the ricotta, then turn out into a 10–12cm ovenproof dish, or on to a piece of baking paper, spreading it out into a 10–12cm diameter circle. Drizzle over 1 tablespoon of the oil and break and sprinkle the rosemary leaves on top, then season with salt and pepper. Place in the air fryer fitted with the basket insert and bake for 10 minutes.

Meanwhile, toss the courgette with salt and the remaining oil and arrange in the air fryer around the disc of ricotta. Bake for a further 8–10 minutes until golden.

To serve, plate up the courgette, sprinkle the pistachios over the ricotta and serve together with some warm focaccia or ciabatta.

HONEY-GLAZED COD WITH LEMON AND GARLIC

Merluzzo alla Sorrentina con aglio, miele e limone

SERVES 4

3 tablespoons honey
Finely grated zest and juice
of 1 lemon
2 tablespoons extra virgin
olive oil
2 tablespoons finely chopped
flat leaf parsley leaves
2 tablespoons oregano leaves
1 small garlic clove, crushed
1 tablespoon chopped
pine nuts
4 skinless cod fillets, about
150g each, at room
temperature
Salt and freshly ground
black pepper

A classic dish from Sorrento on the Amalfi coast. They are famous for their lemons, and, being on the sea, fish is a must-have and it always features some kind of lemon, in a sauce or as a garnish. This is perfect for a light and quick dinner. As you already know, fish is so good for you, so if you are not a huge cod lover, substitute it with salmon or any chunky white fish such as haddock.

Pour the honey and lemon juice into a bowl, and whisk to combine. Gradually add the extra virgin olive oil, stirring continuously. Stir in the lemon zest, parsley, oregano, garlic, pine nuts, ¼ teaspoon salt and ¼ teaspoon pepper.

Gently place the cod fillets in the marinade and spoon it over any pieces that aren't immersed. If you have time, cover and marinate in the fridge for 30 minutes, turning the fish over halfway through. If not, just crack on now.

Preheat the air fryer to 190°C for 3 minutes.

Place a sheet of foil topped with a sheet of baking paper in the air fryer drawer. Gently move the fish around in the marinade, then, using tongs, 2 tablespoons or a spatula, carefully place the cod fillets, skinned side down, on the baking paper. Pour the remaining marinade over the top.

Season with a pinch of salt and pepper then cook for 6 minutes, (they might need a minute less or more, depending how thick your fish fillets are). Serve immediately with a simple salad or my Courgette fries or Butter and bay leaf hasselback potatoes (see pages 64 and 124).

PANZANELLA SALAD WITH KING PRAWNS AND CIABATTA

Insalatona panzanella con gamberoni e ciabatta

SERVES 4

4 teaspoons red wine vinegar
2 tablespoons extra virgin
  olive oil
200g large mixed tomatoes,
  quartered
150g ciabatta, preferably
  3–4 days old, torn into
  bite-sized chunks roughly the
  size of the tomatoes
1 large red onion, finely sliced
1 fennel bulb, finely sliced
80g mixed crispy salad leaves
2 tablespoons roughly
  chopped flat leaf
  parsley leaves
Salt and freshly ground
  black pepper

For the prawns

12 large king prawns, shelled
  and deveined (total weight
  165g)
50g salted butter, cut into
  cubes
½ teaspoon chilli flakes
½ teaspoon sweet (not hot)
  smoked paprika
1 small garlic clove, crushed
Finely grated zest and juice of
  1 lemon

A wonderful healthy Italian salad that is bursting with flavour and will leave you full and satisfied. You can substitute the king prawns with scallops or smaller prawns if you prefer, but you will have to adjust their cooking times slightly. This salad really reminds me of summer, but can be eaten all year round and will never disappoint.

In a large salad bowl or serving dish, use a whisk to mix the vinegar, oil, ½ teaspoon salt and ¼ teaspoon pepper until combined. Add the tomatoes, ciabatta, red onion and fennel, toss well and set aside.

Preheat the air fryer to 200°C for 3 minutes.

Place the prawns in the air fryer drawer and add the butter, chilli, paprika, garlic, lemon zest, ¼ teaspoon salt and ⅛ teaspoon pepper. Mix well, ensuring the prawns are well coated, then cook for 4 minutes. Add the lemon juice and shake to toss the prawns.

Once the prawns are cooked through, remove the drawer from the air fryer and scrape the ciabatta mixture into the drawer. Mix gently with a rubber spatula, so the bread soaks up all the buttery juices.

Transfer everything back to the salad bowl, fold in the salad leaves, sprinkle over the parsley and serve immediately.

COURGETTE FRIES

Zucchine fritte

SERVES 2

20g rice flour, or cornflour
½ teaspoon dried sage
½ teaspoon garlic powder
2 large courgettes, total weight
    about 250g, cut into finger-
    sized fries
1 teaspoon olive oil
Salt and freshly ground
    black pepper
Sea salt flakes

Super-easy to prepare and with huge health benefits, when you compare them to regular fries. These are so versatile and work well with any fish or meat dish, or as party food with drinks, or I've even served them up as a snack while watching a film, instead of popcorn. You can substitute the courgettes with yellow or red peppers, or, even better, a mixture of all three. If you want a little kick, use chilli-infused olive oil instead of olive oil. These are good on their own, or try them with some lemon- or garlic-flavoured mayonnaise for dipping, if you like.

Preheat the air fryer to 200°C for 3 minutes.

In a bowl, mix the rice flour (for extra crispiness), sage, garlic powder, ½ teaspoon salt and ¼ teaspoon pepper. Add the courgette and toss until evenly coated. Drizzle the oil over the courgette and toss well.

Set in the air fryer fitted with the basket insert and cook for 6 minutes. Shake to toss again and cook for a further 6 minutes. Serve immediately, with a sprinkle of sea salt flakes.

PIZZA CHICKEN BREASTS

Pollo alla pizzaiola con mozzarella filante

SERVES 4

60g tomato passata
1 tablespoon tomato purée
1 garlic clove, crushed
¼ teaspoon dried oregano
10 basil leaves, half finely
    chopped, half left whole
4 skinless boneless chicken
    breasts, about 130g each
2 teaspoons olive oil
2 × 125g mozzarella balls,
    drained, excess water gently
    pressed out, finely sliced
Salt and freshly ground
    black pepper

The colour of this recipe makes me smile, as it reminds me of the Italian flag. It is so easy to prepare and full of flavours, and my kids loved it when they were growing up. You can substitute the mozzarella for a good-quality Cheddar or fontina cheese if you prefer, or you can even use a pork chop instead of chicken for a change (though the cooking times will need adjusting).

Preheat your air fryer to 190°C for 3 minutes.

In a small bowl, mix the passata, tomato purée, garlic, oregano, chopped basil and ¼ teaspoon each of salt and pepper and stir with a metal spoon. Set aside.

Rub the chicken breasts with the olive oil and sprinkle over ½ teaspoon salt, then set evenly spaced out in the air fryer fitted with the basket insert. Bake for 6 minutes.

Turn the chicken breasts over carefully with tongs, then equally spread the tomato sauce over each breast, evenly top with mozzarella slices and cook for a further 7 minutes.

Sprinkle over a little pepper, top with the basil leaves and serve.

TOASTED 'RAID THE DELI' PICNIC PANINO

Panino tostato ripieno con giardiniera e affettati

MAKES 2

For the giardiniera relish
60g giardiniera pickle (see recipe introduction)
10–20g mild pickled chillies, to taste
20g small pitted green olives

For the sandwiches
2 ciabatta rolls, or 250g ciabatta loaf, halved horizontally
20g salted butter, or 4 teaspoons olive oil
60g Parma ham slices
60g mortadella slices
60g salami slices
120g sliced Provolone cheese, or good-quality Cheddar
Freshly ground black pepper

Panino with mortadella has to be my favourite panino ever, and, done this way, is just perfection to me. This recipe is fantastic for a quick lunch or picnic: the sharp, spicy pickle is a perfect balance with the salty meats and cheese. You can substitute one of the meats for cooked ham, if you prefer. You can buy jars of giardiniera from any Italian deli. I know that might be a bit of a pain, but honestly, you'll want to make a whole batch of the relish yourself once you try it!

To make the relish, chop the pickle, chillies and olives to make a coarse paste, either in a small food processor or by hand with a sharp knife. Transfer to a small bowl and set aside.

Preheat the air fryer to 190°C for 3 minutes.

Butter the ciabatta, or, if you prefer, pour over a little extra virgin olive oil. Spread the relish over the base slices. Add the meats, then the cheese and sprinkle over some black pepper. Top with the other slice of ciabatta, place in the air fryer fitted with the basket insert and cook for 8 minutes, until the cheese has melted and the ciabatta is browned and crispy.

PIZZA PUFF STICKS

Grissini di sfoglia alla pizzaiola

MAKES 6

25g tomato purée
35g tomato passata
½ teaspoon dried oregano
320g sheet of puff pastry
60g finely grated Parmesan
  cheese
Salt and freshly ground
  black pepper
Sea salt flakes

I would seriously suggest making double batches of these, as they will disappear very quickly. They are a fantastic snack, can be served as canapés, or even to accompany a platter of hams or a soup. They literally last minutes in my house when I make them. You can substitute the Parmesan cheese with any hard cheese, or spread on olive tapenade, which is lovely. If you fancy something sweet, use a chocolate-hazelnut spread such as Nutella directly on the pastry, sprinkle with chopped hazelnuts, fold and twist... You will be very popular that day, trust me!

In a small bowl, with a wooden spoon, mix the tomato purée, passata, oregano, ¼ teaspoon salt and ¼ teaspoon pepper.

Unroll the pastry, leaving it on the paper it came in, then, using a large tablespoon, evenly spread the tomato mixture all over. Now evenly sprinkle over the Parmesan, and fold the sheet of pastry in half to seal in the tomato and cheese.

Cut the pastry into 6 strips, each about 2cm wide. Gently make a twist in middle, a twist at the top and a twist at the bottom. Place them – still on the sheet of baking paper the pastry came in – on a baking tray that fits in the freezer, then freeze for 10 minutes.

Preheat the air fryer to 180°C for 3 minutes.

Put the pizza puff sticks – still on their sheet of baking paper – straight from the freezer into the air fryer fitted with the basket insert, making sure they are well spaced apart, and cook for 12 minutes. (You may need to cook these in batches, if they don't all fit into your air fryer.) Sprinkle over ¼ teaspoon sea salt flakes and some black pepper and serve.

CRISP ROSEMARY-CRUSTED PORK LOIN CHOPS

Lombo di maiale alla Milanese

SERVES 4

1 large egg
150g fine dried breadcrumbs
1 tablespoon olive oil
2½ tablespoons finely
   chopped rosemary leaves
   (about 6 rosemary sprigs)
4 thick pork loin steaks, about
   175g each
Salt and freshly ground
   black pepper

Whenever it's just me and my eldest son Luciano at home, this is our go-to boys' night dinner, served with a fresh crispy green salad and a cold beer each: the perfect night. Like most of the recipes in this book, it's an easy dish to scale up or down to suit the number of mouths you have to feed. You can also make this with chicken breasts if you prefer, and, if you fancy a little kick, substitute the black pepper with chilli powder. The crispy breadcrumb crust keeps the meat really tender inside.

Lightly beat the egg in a bowl and set aside.

Place the breadcrumbs, oil, rosemary, ½ teaspoon salt and ½ teaspoon pepper in a wide flat bowl or tray. Mix together using your fingertips, as you would when making crumble, until combined.

Working with 1 pork loin steak at a time, dip first in the breadcrumbs, pressing lightly on both sides, then shake off any excess. Dip the steak into the egg, immersing it to fully cover the meat on both sides. Then again coat in the breadcrumbs, ensuring it's completely covered and pressing the crumbs lightly into any missed patches. Set on a tray and repeat the process with the remaining pork steaks.

Preheat the air fryer to 180°C for 3 minutes.

Set the breaded steaks in your air fryer fitted with the basket insert and cook for 12 minutes, (add 3 minutes if your steaks are really thick), until golden and cooked through. Serve with seasonal greens or a crisp green salad and – if you're like my kids – creamy mash too!

CHICKEN INVOLTINI WITH HAM AND SMOKED MOZZARELLA

Involtini di pollo con prosciutto e formaggio

SERVES 4

2 large skinless chicken breasts,
    total weight about 500g
80g cooked ham slices
150g scamorza cheese,
    finely sliced
35g panko breadcrumbs
1 tablespoon olive oil
4 lemon wedges
4 bay leaves
Salt and freshly ground
    black pepper

My kids absolutely love this recipe, and, to be honest, if I do serve them with salad as the recipe suggests, rather than something more substantial and carby, I have to make double the amount as everyone wants two each. This is a really easy, quick way to make stuffed chicken parcels. I tend to make them in the morning, then pop them in the fridge and just cook them when they're needed. Because the breast is rolled, no fiddly instructions are needed to create the stuffing. You can substitute the cooked ham with mortadella and the scamorza with mozzarella, if you prefer.

Place the chicken breasts on a work surface and slice them in half horizontally (parallel to the work surface), to create 4 long, flat portions.

Season the chicken with a pinch each of salt and pepper, place a slice of ham on each piece, then evenly lay the scamorza slices on top. Roll from a short side, then tighten and secure the roll with a couple of cocktail sticks. Repeat to form all the rolls.

Place the breadcrumbs in a wide, shallow bowl and the olive oil in another small bowl. Dip the chicken parcels first in the oil and then roll them in the breadcrumbs, coating them completely. With dry hands, press the crumbs lightly into any missed patches, to give a lovely even crust.

Preheat the air fryer to 180°C for 3 minutes.

Line the air fryer basket insert with baking paper, then place in all the chicken parcels. Add the lemon wedges and bay leaves in between. Cook for 20 minutes.

Remove the cocktail sticks, place a chicken parcel on each plate and serve with a large handful of your favourite crispy salad.

ROASTED STUFFED PEPPERS WITH BOLOGNESE SAUCE AND MOZZARELLA

Peperoni ripieni con sugo alla Bolognese e mozzarella

SERVES 2

2 large peppers, about
    260g each
2 teaspoons olive oil
400g homemade Bolognese
    sauce (see page 23)
125g mozzarella ball, drained
    and cut into 4 slices
Salt and freshly ground
    black pepper

If you have any leftover Bolognese sauce, or have someone in your house who is carb-free or gluten-free, this is the perfect recipe to serve them. We were in exactly that situation once in Sardinia when a guest arrived. I quickly adapted his dinner to make this for him... and the rest of us were really jealous as it looked so good. It is absolutely delicious and so filling. You can be as creative as you like; I've even stuffed peppers with leftover risotto (see page 33 for an air fryer risotto recipe) which is also a must-try. Please only use red, orange or yellow peppers, for a sweeter taste.

Slice the tops off the peppers to make lids about 2.5cm deep, then scoop the seeds out and discard. Rub the lids and peppers with the olive oil and rub with ¼ teaspoon salt and ⅛ teaspoon pepper.

Preheat the air fryer to 170°C for 3 minutes.

Fill the peppers evenly with half the Bolognese sauce, then place a smaller slice of mozzarella on top. Continue to fill the pepper with the remaining Bolognese. Place the peppers in the air fryer fitted with the basket insert, put their stalk lids on top and cook for 15 minutes.

Remove the pepper lids, top each pepper with a remaining slice of mozzarella and continue to cook for a final 5 minutes until the cheese is bubbling and melting. Serve with their lids and salad.

CRISPY CHICKPEAS WITH GARLIC AND FENNEL SEEDS

Ceci croccanti con aglio e finocchietto

SERVES 4

400g can of chickpeas, drained and rinsed
20g rice flour, or cornflour
½ tablespoon finely chopped rosemary leaves
½ teaspoon garlic powder
½ teaspoon fennel seeds, roughly crushed
1 teaspoon cumin seeds
2 teaspoons extra virgin olive oil
Salt and freshly ground black pepper
Sea salt flakes

Who doesn't love a bar snack? There is something quite special about making your own, and these are perfect with an ice-cold negroni, or a Martini Bianco on ice. Keep them in an airtight container to stay lovely and crisp for longer, though I doubt there will be any left once you start eating them. I sometimes like to make them spicy by adding 1 teaspoon of chilli powder along with the other flavourings, so give that a go if you like it hot. Rice flour will make these especially crispy.

Preheat the air fryer to 180°C for 3 minutes.

Tip the chickpeas on to a plate lined with kitchen paper and make sure they are as dry as you can get them.

Mix the rice flour, rosemary, garlic, fennel, cumin, ¼ teaspoon salt and ½ teaspoon pepper in a bowl, add the dried chickpeas and toss well to coat evenly. Pour over the oil and toss again to roughly coat.

Tip into the air fryer drawer and cook for 14–16 minutes, shaking to toss halfway through, until golden and crispy. Sprinkle with sea salt flakes, then allow to cool. Serve them up with your favourite drinks.

My motto is work hard, play hard, but always remember what it is all for: family! To me, there is nothing better than sitting down with my family and enjoying a meal. When I'm home, The D'Acampos sit down together as a family most nights, phones are banned and we spend just an hour with each other, really talking and enjoying the moment. I am a true believer that this is why my family is so close and my boys – who are now grown men – still choose to spend so much time with us. It really is a moment in the day that we all treasure.

With some of these recipes, you can substitute the main ingredient as long as you stick to the same method, because they are very versatile. Nonna Assunta's pork rib recipe can be made with chicken drumsticks, for instance, while the chicken in the burgers can of course be substituted with a meat or fish of your choice and will still be fantastic.

I really urge you to try the whole cauliflower, which works with any main meal. It looks so impressive, is so quick and easy to prepare and just delicious. Another of my favourites is the gnocchi in pancetta and tomato sauce. Gnocchi goes way back to Roman times and yet oddly still isn't yet a family meal go-to in this country, though it is filling, so quick to make and gives you an alternative to pasta.

These recipes are firm favourites with my family, but they are also fantastic for when you have friends over. They are really wholesome, tasty and nearly as good as a cuddle. (Let's be honest, who doesn't want a bit of that a couple of times a week?) Family time with healthy comfort food, such as my golden croquettes, carbonara potatoes, amazing sausage rolls or Scotch eggs, is like a secret medicine that lifts me up for the rest of the week. I hope it has the same effect on you.

FAMILY

BAKED PASTA WITH SAUSAGES, GARLIC, ROSEMARY AND MOZZARELLA

Pasta al forno

SERVES 4

400g pork sausages
1 fennel bulb, chopped
  (reserve the fronds)
2 tablespoons olive oil
1 large garlic clove, crushed
1 heaped teaspoon finely
  chopped rosemary leaves, or
  ½ teaspoon dried rosemary
1 level teaspoon fennel seeds
¼ teaspoon chilli flakes, or
  Calabrian chilli paste from
  a jar, or to taste
300g dried paccheri or
  rigatoni pasta
400g can of chopped
  tomatoes
350g tomato passata
1 tablespoon finely chopped
  flat leaf parsley leaves
125g mozzarella ball, drained
  and roughly torn
Salt and freshly ground
  black pepper

Who doesn't love a pasta bake? This recipe reminds me of when my kids used to come home, freezing, from playing a sport in the crazy cold weather of the UK fields in winter and were so grateful to be served this. Please use good-quality sausages, and, if you can get the Italian-style with fennel, even better. Boil the pasta only until it is very al dente, for at least three minutes less than instructed on the packet.

Preheat the air fryer to 180°C for 3 minutes.

Squeeze the sausagemeat out of the skins and into a 23cm diameter oven dish, or directly into the air fryer drawer, if yours is the same size. Add the chopped fennel and oil, mix with your hands to break up the meat then cook for 8 minutes. Add 2 teaspoons water, the garlic, rosemary, fennel seeds and chilli, mix well and cook for a further 5 minutes.

Meanwhile, pour 3 litres water into a large saucepan with 1 tablespoon salt, bring to the boil, then place in your pasta. Cook the pasta, stirring occasionally, for 3 minutes less than instructed by the packet, so it's very al dente (remember it will continue to cook in the air fryer). Drain.

Reduce the air fryer temperature to 160°C.

Add the chopped tomatoes to the sausagemeat mixture with the passata, parsley, 1 teaspoon salt, ½ teaspoon pepper and the drained pasta, mix together using a wooden spoon and cook for 10 minutes.

Stir again, top with the torn mozzarella and cook for a final 10 minutes until golden and crispy on top. Allow to rest for a couple of minutes, then serve.

DEVILLED CHICKEN WINGS WITH SMOKED PAPRIKA AND HONEY

Ali di pollo alla diavola caramellizzate al miele

SERVES 4

1kg chicken wings
75g honey
1–3 tablespoons Calabrian
    chilli paste from a jar, or
    jarred chopped chillies,
    to taste
1½ teaspoons red wine
    vinegar
1 tablespoon tomato purée
1 tablespoon olive oil
1 teaspoon garlic powder
40g rice flour, or cornflour
1 teaspoon sweet smoked
    paprika
50g 'nduja from a jar
150g mascarpone, or
    Dolcelatte
Salt and freshly ground
    black pepper

My boys Luciano and Rocco absolutely love this, especially when they are watching a film and want easy finger food. The Calabrian chilli paste gives a sweet, smoky and very spicy flavour, and, together with the mascarpone which cools that down, the flavours are really a match made in heaven. You can make the wings as spicy as you like by simply adding more chilli or 'nduja, or you can substitute the honey with maple syrup, or the mascarpone with cream cheese, if you like.

Place the chicken wings in a colander, mix in 1 teaspoon salt and let the skin dry out for 15 minutes while you get everything else ready.

To make the marinade, pour the honey into a large bowl and add the chilli paste or chopped chillies, vinegar, tomato purée and oil. Mix using a whisk, then set aside.

Preheat the air fryer to 190°C for 3 minutes.

In another large bowl, mix the garlic powder, flour, paprika and ½ teaspoon pepper, add the chicken wings and toss to get them evenly coated. Pour about three-quarters of the honey marinade over the chicken and mix well. Transfer to the air fryer fitted with the basket insert and cook for 10 minutes. Turn the wings and cook for a further 8 minutes until sticky and cooked through.

Meanwhile mix the 'nduja with the remaining marinade. Drizzle the sauce mixture on top of the wings and cook for a final 1–2 minutes to melt. Plate up, dot with the mascarpone or Dolcelatte and serve with an ice-cold beer or a glass of full-bodied red wine.

FOUR CHEESE MACCHERONI WITH EXTRA-CRISPY TOPPING

Maccheroni ai quattro formaggi

SERVES 4

25g plain flour
250ml whole milk
175g mascarpone
150g Gorgonzola cheese
½ teaspoon freshly grated
   nutmeg
100g grated Parmesan cheese
300g dried cavatappi or
   rigatoni pasta
125g mozzarella ball, drained
Salt and freshly ground
   black pepper

The ultimate comfort food. When this is served to you, it's as if you are getting a huge cuddle... and what could be better than that? You can substitute the Gorgonzola with Taleggio or Dolcelatte, if you prefer, and I like to add peas sometimes for a bit of colour, sweetness and texture (just add 100g peas when stirring in the Parmesan). You're welcome x

Mix the flour in a cup with about 100ml of the milk until smooth.

Place a saucepan over a medium heat, add the mascarpone and stir using a whisk. Once melted, crumble in the Gorgonzola. When the Gorgonzola has melted and the mix is bubbling gently, pour in the milk and flour mixture from the cup, the rest of the milk, the nutmeg and ½ teaspoon black pepper.

Increase the heat slightly and keep stirring until the mixture thickens slightly, about 3 minutes. Add half the Parmesan cheese and mix well, then turn off the heat.

Bring 3 litres of water to the boil, add 1 tablespoon salt and cook the pasta for 2 minutes less than instructed on the packet. Drain it well, then stir the pasta into the sauce until well coated.

Preheat the air fryer to 180°C for 3 minutes. Tip the pasta into a deep, 20cm diameter baking dish and bake for 10 minutes.

Meanwhile, gently squeeze the mozzarella ball to remove as much liquid as possible, then tear it into pieces.

Reduce the air fryer temperature to 160°C. Place the torn mozzarella on top of the pasta, sprinkle with the rest of the Parmesan and bake for a final 20 minutes, or until golden and bubbling.

SUCCULENT CHICKEN BURGERS WITH ROCKET AND PARMESAN

Burgers di pollo con rucola e parmigiano

SERVES 4

4 small skin-on chicken breasts
40g unsalted butter, softened
80g Parmesan cheese, 60g
   finely grated, 20g shaved
4 brioche burger buns, halved
40g mayonnaise
4 handfuls of rocket leaves
½ lemon
Salt and freshly ground
   black pepper

Who doesn't love a cheeky chicken burger? Cooking these in an air fryer works brilliantly, because the cheesy, buttery juices from the burgers are absolutely delicious on the brioche buns. You can substitute chicken with pieces of cod if you fancy. If you do decide to make a cod burger, substitute the Parmesan with breadcrumbs and please make my fantastic Super-crispy polenta chips with salsa tonnata (see page 165) to go with it, as the tuna sauce works perfectly with both!

Preheat your air fryer to 200°C for 3 minutes.

Brush or rub the chicken breasts with the butter to coat. Set on a silicone air fryer liner, or on a small sheet of baking paper, sprinkle over the grated Parmesan cheese, ¼ teaspoon salt and ½ teaspoon pepper, shake off the excess, turn over and press to coat the other sides, ensuring you mop up all the last bits.

Place in the air fryer fitted with the basket insert, paper or liner and all, space out evenly and bake for 14 minutes until golden and cooked through. (If your chicken breasts are thin, cook them for 1–2 minutes less, and, if thick, for 1–2 minutes more.) Baste with the buttery juices halfway through cooking.

Once the chicken breasts are cooked, remove them from the air fryer and let them rest and keep warm while you toast the buns. Brush the cut sides of the buns with the buttery juices from the chicken and air fry for 4–5 minutes.

To create the ultimate chicken burger, spread some mayonnaise on the base of the buns (my sons like a little mustard or sweet chilli sauce too) and place a chicken breast on top of each with a handful of rocket leaves. Squeeze a little lemon juice over the leaves and top with the Parmesan shavings. Don't forget to mop up any crispy cheesy bits from the paper or liner too! Serve straight away.

SCOTCH EGG WITH MARTINI BIANCO

Polpette di carne al Martini Bianco ripiene d'uovo

MAKES 6

8 eggs, at room temperature

300g minced pork

300g minced lamb

40ml Martini Bianco, or Cinzano (or see recipe introduction)

3 pitted green olives, finely chopped, plus 1 tablespoon of their brine from the jar

¼ teaspoon freshly grated nutmeg

1 tablespoon chopped flat leaf parsley leaves

2 teaspoons chopped chives

30g finely grated Parmesan cheese

90g dried breadcrumbs

2 tablespoons olive oil

Salt and freshly ground black pepper

I will never forget the first time I ate a Scotch egg, at my mother-in-law Liz's house. I was expecting to bite into an arancine ball and didn't understand how she could get it so wrong... where was the rice? And yet, she got it so right, as it tasted amazing. I was fully converted in minutes and now they are a favourite snack when I have a poker night with my boys! You can definitely cook this recipe without alcohol, just replace it with whole milk, and of course you can substitute the minced pork or lamb with beef, if you prefer. For me, they are amazing any time of the day, including breakfast. Top tip? Make a double batch!

Preheat the air fryer to 150°C for 3 minutes.

Put 6 of the eggs in the air fryer fitted with the basket insert and cook for 8–9 minutes for softer centres and 13 minutes for hard-boiled. Gently place in a bowl of ice-cold water to cool down for 5 minutes, then peel. (The longer you leave them, the harder they will be to peel.)

Place both types of minced meat in a large bowl with the Martini, olives and their brine, nutmeg, parsley, chives, Parmesan cheese, ½ teaspoon salt and ¼ teaspoon pepper. Mix well with your hand until combined.

Wet your hands to stop the meat mixture from sticking, then divide it into 6 equal balls. Flatten each into a disc in the palm of your hand. Place a boiled egg in the middle, then with the help of your other hand mould the meat around the egg, completely encasing it. Shape into a neat ball and set aside. Repeat the process with the remaining meat mixture and eggs.

Increase the air fryer temperature to 180°C.

Crack the remaining 2 eggs into a bowl and beat with a fork. Put the breadcrumbs in a separate bowl with 1 tablespoon of the oil and mix with your fingertips as you would when making a crumble.

One at a time, gently roll the Scotch eggs in the breadcrumbs, shaking off any excess crumbs, then dip into the beaten egg, then place back in the breadcrumbs, pressing them lightly into any missed patches.

Set them in the air fryer fitted with the basket insert, drizzle or spray with the remaining oil and cook for 20 minutes. You're welcome!

CRISP CHEESY AUBERGINE BITES

Bocconcini croccanti di melanzane e formaggio

MAKES 12

1–2 aubergines, total weight about 750g
4 teaspoons olive oil
50g dried breadcrumbs
25g plain flour
1 egg, lightly beaten
70g finely grated pecorino Romano cheese, plus more to serve
Finely grated zest of 1 small lemon, plus lemon wedges to serve
Salt and freshly ground black pepper

This recipe always makes me smile. My mother used to cook these instead of meatballs, to encourage us to eat more vegetables. I loved them, but I always remember my sister complaining about them and giving me most of her share under the table. It's funny how persistence works, as it is now one of her favourite recipes to eat and prepare and she serves it to her kids, trying (you guessed it!) to get them to eat more vegetables... These cute bites are fantastic as a snack or to go with a favourite barbecue dish.

Preheat the air fryer to 180°C for 3 minutes.

Peel strips of skin off the aubergine, so it is striped black and white, then cut it into 2cm cubes. Toss the aubergine cubes with 2 teaspoons of the olive oil and ½ teaspoon salt. Cook in the air fryer fitted with the basket insert for 13 minutes. Shake to toss well, then cook for a further 10 minutes until the aubergine is golden and cooked through. Remove and allow to cool completely.

Pour the breadcrumbs into a bowl, pour in 1 teaspoon of oil and mix using your fingertips as you would when making a crumble..

Pour the flour into a separate bowl with 1 teaspoon water, the egg, pecorino cheese, half the lemon zest, ¼ teaspoon salt and ¼ teaspoon pepper. Mix well using a whisk or fork until smooth. Add the aubergine chunks and mix. The mixture will be a sticky, chunky paste.

One at a time, shape the aubergine mixture into balls, making 12 in total. Place in the bowl of breadcrumbs and gently roll, ensuring all the balls are well coated and pressing the crumbs lightly into any missed patches.

Increase the air fryer temperature to 200°C.

Set the balls in the air fryer fitted with the basket insert, drizzle over the remaining 1 teaspoon olive oil, then cook for 12 minutes until golden, tossing halfway through. To serve, sprinkle over the remaining lemon zest and some shavings of pecorino cheese and add the lemon wedges.

CREAMY FISH PIE WITH PARSLEY, GARLIC AND LEMON GREMOLATA

Torta salata di pesce con gremolata

SERVES 4

3 eggs
3 tablespoons finely chopped
flat leaf parsley leaves
1 garlic clove, crushed
Finely grated zest of 1 lemon
300g skinless cod fillet
160g skinless undyed smoked
haddock fillet
100g large cooked prawns,
peeled and deveined
25g plain flour
225ml whole milk
100ml double cream
½ teaspoon freshly grated
nutmeg
Salt and freshly ground
black pepper

For the topping
450g floury potatoes, such as
Maris Piper, scrubbed
Olive oil, or olive oil spray
20g finely grated Grana
Padano cheese

Fish pies are just wonderful and you can be as creative as you like with them, depending on what fish you buy. I often use salmon instead of cod, for example. I knew gremolata would be fantastic in this recipe: it cuts through the rich sauce perfectly. You can eat this dish as is, but I like to serve it with a simple mixed salad dressed with extra virgin olive oil, lemon juice, salt and pepper.

Preheat your air fryer to 150°C for 3 minutes.

Put the eggs in the air fryer fitted with the basket insert and cook for 8–9 minutes. Gently place in a small bowl of ice-cold water to cool down for 5 minutes, then peel and halve.

In a small bowl, mix the parsley, garlic and lemon zest to make the gremolata. Set aside.

Increase the air fryer temperature to 180°C. Slice the potatoes about 5mm thick, toss them in 1 tablespoon oil and cook for 10 minutes, tossing halfway through. Tip them on to a plate.

Meanwhile, roughly slice the fish into chunks and place in a deep, round ovenproof dish (about 20cm in diameter and 6cm deep), or directly into the air fryer drawer, if yours is the same size. Add the prawns. Sprinkle over three-quarters of the gremolata, ¼ teaspoon salt and ¼ teaspoon pepper and mix well with your hands.

Pour the flour and 50ml of the milk into a small saucepan over a medium heat. Using a whisk, stir until smooth (about 1 minute). Add the remaining milk, the cream, nutmeg, ½ teaspoon salt and ½ teaspoon pepper. Reduce the heat to low and cook for 8 minutes until it thickens. Pour the sauce over the fish and place in the egg halves.

Reduce the air fryer temperature to 170°C. Top the pie with an even layer of the potatoes, then brush or spray a little more olive oil over the slices and bake for 20 minutes, or until golden, bubbling and cooked through. Sprinkle the Grana Padano cheese on top and bake for a final 10 minutes.

Remove from the air fryer, sprinkle over the remaining gremolata to add a zing and serve immediately.

MORTADELLA, SOUR CHERRY, FONTINA AND RED ONION SAUSAGE ROLLS

Rotolino di salsiccia con mortadella e cipolle rosse

MAKES 6

20g dried sour cherries, halved
1 small Tropea onion, or
    ½ red onion, finely chopped
60g mortadella, chopped into
    5mm pieces
300g herby pork sausages,
    skinned
25g fresh white breadcrumbs
50g fontina cheese, cut into
    tiny cubes
1½ tablespoons finely
    chopped flat leaf
    parsley leaves
½ teaspoon chilli flakes
320g sheet of puff pastry
1 egg yolk, lightly beaten with
    a pinch of salt
2 teaspoons fennel seeds
Salt and freshly ground
    black pepper
Sea salt flakes

The rich cheese and pork flavours balance with the cherries here. These are thick sausage rolls, so the pastry has time to get nice and golden while the filling doesn't dry out. You can substitute mortadella with cooked ham, or even do without either. These are perfect for when the kids come back from school, or to serve at a party. When we have a family picnic, my wife always cooks them.

Place the cherries in a small heatproof bowl, pour over 2 tablespoons boiling water and leave for 10 minutes so they can plump up. Drain away any excess water.

In a large bowl, put the onion, mortadella, sausagemeat, breadcrumbs, cheese, parsley, chilli flakes, drained cherries, ½ teaspoon salt and ¼ teaspoon pepper. Mix well with your hands.

Unroll the puff pastry sheet with a long side facing you and cut a 6cm strip from the top. (Wrap then freeze this for future use.) Cut the remaining pastry into 2 halves. Shape the filling into 2 sausages as long as the length of the pastry rectangles. Place each at one side of a pastry sheet, leaving a 2cm border from the sausagemeat filling to the edge. Brush the border with a little of the beaten egg yolk and fold the other side of the pastry over to seal the filling in and give a seam on one side. Press the 2 pieces of pastry along each seam with a fork, to seal.

Leave the sausage rolls in the freezer to firm up for 20 minutes.

Preheat the air fryer to 190°C for 3 minutes.

Using a very sharp knife, trim a little off the ends of each roll to neaten. Cut each roll into 3 even pieces. Brush the pastry with the remaining egg yolk and sprinkle over the fennel seeds and a few sea salt flakes.

Place the sausage rolls in the air fryer fitted with the basket insert, spaced apart, and cook for 25–30 minutes until the pastry is golden and the filling is cooked through. Serve hot, or at room temperature.

CARBONARA POTATOES

Patate al forno stile carbonara con guanciale e parmigiano

SERVES 4

850g floury potatoes, such as
  Maris Piper, scrubbed and
  sliced about 5mm thick
  (a mandoline works well)
300ml double cream
1 small garlic clove, sliced
1 bay leaf
1 tablespoon olive oil
70g guanciale, chopped
60g finely grated Parmesan
  cheese
Salt and freshly ground
  black pepper

At first glance, this might just look like a potato bake, but because of the guanciale and cheese, it really is a meal in itself and you don't need to add anything to it except a side of greens or salad. This is my son Rocco's favourite way to eat potatoes; he always asked my mum Alba to make them for him, and now, when I serve it up, it's as if she is sitting with us, which is so nice... I love how food can bring back wonderful memories. You can substitute the guanciale with pancetta, if you prefer.

Pour 2 litres water into a large saucepan with 1 tablespoon salt and bring to the boil. Add the potato slices and cook for about 5 minutes until they are tender; don't let them over cook. Drain in a colander and allow to cool slightly.

Put the cream, garlic, bay leaf, ¼ teaspoon salt and ¼ teaspoon pepper in the empty saucepan and place over a high heat. Once it gets close to boiling, reduce the heat to low and leave to infuse for 5 minutes. Remove from the heat, take out the bay leaf and set aside.

Oil a dish which fits in the air fryer with the 1 tablespoon oil. Layer about one-third of the potatoes in the dish, then sprinkle over one-third each of the guanciale, Parmesan and cream, with a pinch of salt and pepper. Repeat the process as you build the layers, but don't use the final third of the Parmesan on the top just yet. Press the whole thing down with your hands, to compact it slightly.

Preheat the air fryer to 160°C for 3 minutes.

Cover the potato bake loosely with a sheet of foil. It shouldn't touch the top of the potatoes, but you can seal it loosely around the dish so it stays firmly in place. Cook for 15 minutes.

Remove the foil and cook for 15 minutes, then top with the remaining Parmesan cheese and some black pepper, Cook for a final 15 minutes until golden and bubbling. Remove from the air fryer and let stand for 5 minutes before serving.

APRICOT AND ROSEMARY GLAZED CHICKEN

Pollo arrosto con rosmarino e marmellata di albicocche

SERVES 4–6

1 medium whole chicken,
   about 1.8kg, removed from
   the fridge about 1 hour
   before cooking
1 lemon, halved
3 rosemary sprigs
25ml olive oil
½ teaspoon fennel seeds,
   roughly crushed
20g apricot jam (or see
   recipe introduction)
Salt and freshly ground
   black pepper

Roast chicken is loved by all, and it is so versatile, too. You can eat it hot with all the trimmings, or leave it to cool, then shred it and enjoy in a salad or sandwich. Either way, it's a winner. The great thing about cooking a chicken in an air fryer is that the heat is really concentrated, so the skin crisps up nicely but still leaves the meat really tender. You can substitute the apricot jam for honey, if you prefer. Enjoy!

Preheat the air fryer to 180°C for 3 minutes.

Dab the chicken skin dry with kitchen paper, then fill its cavity with the lemon halves and 1 rosemary sprig. Rub the skin all over using 1 tablespoon of the olive oil. Sprinkle over the fennel seeds, salt and pepper and place the other rosemary sprigs on each leg of the bird.

Line the air fryer drawer with baking paper, or a silicone liner. Place the chicken breast side down directly in the lined air fryer drawer and roast for 20 minutes.

Carefully turn the chicken over and roast for a further 15 minutes.

Brush the apricot jam and remaining oil all over the chicken skin, increase the air fryer temperature to 190°C and roast for a final 10–20 minutes, or until the chicken is cooked through and the skin is caramelised.

Place on a serving plate, drizzling over any juices, and serve with my favourite Butter and bay leaf hasselback potatoes (see page 124), or with any salad or vegetables your family prefers.

ROMAN-STYLE PIZZA WITH OLIVES AND SEMI-DRIED TOMATOES

Pizza alla Romana con mozzarella, olive e pomodori semi-secchi

SERVES 2

For the base
1 teaspoon dried yeast
½ teaspoon runny honey
150ml lukewarm water
175g strong white bread flour
1 teaspoon fine sea salt
2½ tablespoons olive oil, plus
   more for your fingers

For the topping
2 tablespoons tomato passata
1 tablespoon tomato purée
1 tablespoon chilli oil
125g mozzarella ball, drained
   and torn
10 pitted green olives in
   brine, drained
5 basil leaves
5–6 semi-dried tomatoes in
   oil, drained
Salt and freshly ground
   black pepper

This is a great recipe if you want to get the kids involved in cooking. You can use any toppings you prefer, as you would on any pizza. This particular recipe isn't a classic Neapolitan pizza, but it's still very delicious: Roman-style pizza has a characteristically crispy bottom and crispy crust. I always serve pizza with chilled Italian beer, but obviously not to the kids! You can substitute the semi-dried tomatoes with halved red or yellow cherry tomatoes, or a few slices of roasted peppers from a jar, if you prefer.

In a bowl, mix the yeast, honey and measured lukewarm water, then leave it for 10 minutes until it gets creamy and lightly foamy on top. Add the flour and salt and mix with a rubber spatula until the mixture combines to make a shaggy dough. Spoon 2 tablespoons of the oil into a 19cm diameter round cake tin, then tip the dough in. Turn the dough over to coat it all over in the oil, cover loosely with clingfilm, then leave somewhere warm to double in size (this will take about 1¼ hours).

Once the dough has risen, oil the tips of your fingers, then nip the dough from the outside and pull out to stretch a little, then fold back on to itself, lightly pressing the end you grabbed into the middle. Do this 4 times, all the way around, to make a plump ball. Drizzle the rest of the oil over, cover and leave somewhere warm again to double in size. Again, it will take about 1¼ hours.

Preheat the air fryer to 200°C for 3 minutes.

Using your fingertips, gently massage the dough to push it to the edges of the cake tin to create a thick 3cm crust and a slightly thinner middle section. Cook for 12 minutes.

Meanwhile, mix the tomato passata and purée in a small bowl with ¼ teaspoon salt and ⅛ teaspoon pepper. Spread the tomato mixture in the middle of the pizza base, leaving the 3cm crust bare, drizzle with the chilli oil and dot the mozzarella, olives, basil and tomatoes on top.

Cook for a further 5 minutes, then serve straight away.

WHOLE ROAST CAULIFLOWER WITH CALABRIAN CHILLIES AND LEMON ZEST

Cavolfiore intero arrostito con peperoncini Calabresi e scorzetta di limone

SERVES 4

1 large cauliflower, about
   700g
70g salted butter, at room
   temperature
50g finely grated Parmesan
   cheese
Finely grated zest of 1 lemon,
   plus the juice of ½
1 tablespoon Calabrian
   chilli paste from a jar,
   or 50g 'nduja from a jar
Salt and freshly ground
   black pepper

This recipe is amazing either as a main meal for two, or as a side dish to accompany any meat or fish. If you can't find Calabrian chilli paste or 'nduja (though they will be stocked in jars in larger supermarkets), you can substitute with chilli oil. I particularly love this dish on a barbecue day. It's a very easy recipe to prepare and cook, fantastic for air fryer beginners, or for those cooking a difficult meal who need a quick and easy accompaniment. Another bonus: it's mess-free, so there's very little washing-up to do.

Preheat the air fryer to 200°C for 3 minutes.

Cut off the stem from the cauliflower and cut away the tough core from underneath, by slicing out a reverse cone shape, being careful to leave the cauliflower intact as a whole. (You need to remove it so that the remaining cauliflower cooks more quickly and evenly.) Remove any tough leaves, but leave the rest on, then rub all over with the butter and sprinkle with ½ teaspoon salt and ¼ teaspoon pepper.

Place the cauliflower in the air fryer fitted with the basket insert and cook for 15 minutes.

Sprinkle over the Parmesan cheese and lemon zest and dot the chilli paste or 'nduja on top. Cook for a further 5 minutes.

Squeeze over the lemon juice and baste with the cooking juices, then serve immediately.

GNOCCHI IN PANCETTA, TOMATO AND PARMESAN SAUCE

Gnocchi in salsa di pomodoro con pancetta e parmigiano

SERVES 4

150g pancetta lardons

1 large garlic clove, crushed

2 × 400g cans of chopped tomatoes

2 tablespoons tomato purée

10 basil leaves

80g finely grated Parmesan cheese

800g good-quality shop-bought potato gnocchi

Salt and freshly ground black pepper

This is my daughter Mia's favourite way to cook and eat gnocchi and she could make this recipe all by herself when she was just 10 years old, with my supervision of course. Please make sure you buy the best-quality gnocchi you can afford, to get the best results. As soon as they all float to the surface of the boiling water, they are ready to drain. You can substitute the pancetta with chopped courgettes, and the Parmesan with a vegetarian hard cheese, if you prefer.

Preheat the air fryer to 170°C for 3 minutes.

Put the pancetta in the air fryer drawer and cook for 7 minutes until crispy, stir in the garlic and cook for another minute. Pour in all the chopped tomatoes and add the tomato purée, basil, half the Parmesan, ½ teaspoon salt and ¼ teaspoon pepper.

Mix well using a wooden spoon, increase the air fryer temperature to 190°C and cook for 20 minutes. Stir occasionally.

In a large saucepan, bring 3 litres water to the boil with 1 teaspoon salt. Cook the gnocchi according to the packet instructions, then drain, tip the gnocchi into the air fryer drawer over the sauce and mix gently but well. Top with the remaining Parmesan cheese and cook for 10 minutes. Plate up and serve immediately.

SMASHED POTATOES WITH SPECK HAM AND GORGONZOLA

Patate schiacciate con speck e Gorgonzola

SERVES 4

800g new potatoes, or other small waxy potatoes
20g salted butter, cut into cubes
1 tablespoon olive oil
90g Gorgonzola cheese, chopped
50g sliced speck ham
6 sage leaves
Salt and freshly ground black pepper

My wife says that she could eat this as a main meal every day, and you will often catch her with a bowl full, topped with sour cream and chives. But personally, I see this dish more as a sharing starter, or as an accompaniment to something. My favourite way of eating it is for breakfast or brunch, topped with a fried egg… it's honestly heaven. So I guess anything goes really! You can substitute the speck with Parma ham if you prefer, and, if you fancy a little kick, just add a sprinkle of chilli powder on top.

Pour 2 litres water into a large saucepan with 1 tablespoon salt, place in the potatoes and bring to the boil. Boil until the potatoes are just softened and tender (they should fall off when you stick a knife in and lift them); it should take 15–20 minutes in total.

Drain the potatoes, then tip them back in to the pan to dry out a little.

Place the butter and oil in the air fryer drawer and preheat to 190°C for 3 minutes.

Take the air fryer drawer out, place in the potatoes and toss them in the butter mixture, along with ¼ teaspoon salt and ½ teaspoon pepper. Gently press each potato with a potato masher or fork to roughly open them, then cook for 15 minutes.

Turn the potatoes and cook for a further 5 minutes until golden.

Turn the potatoes once more, dot over the cheese, speck and sage and cook for a final 5–8 minutes until crispy-melty. So delicious!

BRANDIED TURKEY BREAST

Petto di tacchino al burro e brandy

SERVES 8

1 medium-sized turkey breast, about 1.8kg
1 onion, cut into 2cm-thick rounds

For the brine

3 litres water
2 teaspoons caraway seeds
2 teaspoons black peppercorns
2 teaspoons juniper berries
5 thyme sprigs
3 bay leaves
Pared zest of 1 lemon, removed in broad strips with a vegetable peeler
75g fine sea salt
60g golden caster sugar

For the butter

85g salted butter, at room temperature
1 tablespoon golden caster sugar
1 tablespoon brandy
Leaves from 3 thyme sprigs, finely chopped
Salt and freshly ground black pepper

For the gravy

15g salted butter
1 tablespoon plain flour
100ml white wine
700ml chicken stock

A question I'm always asked – especially around Christmas – is how to keep turkey moist, as it's such a lean meat. That made it a challenge to cook in an air fryer... until I came up with this brining technique, which really helps. Don't be put off by the long list of ingredients: like many of my recipes, it's still super-easy to prepare.

You will need to brine the turkey overnight. Place all the brine ingredients except for half the water in a large saucepan and place over a medium heat until starting to steam, then reduce the heat and leave to infuse over a low heat for 20 minutes. Take off the heat and pour into a large bowl or pot that will fit in the fridge, with the remaining water (be sure there is still room to fit in the turkey). Leave to cool completely. Gently submerge the turkey in the brine: it needs to be fully covered, so top up with water if needed. Cover and chill for at least 12 hours, 24 would be even better.

Carefully lift the turkey out of the brine (discard the brine and spices). Dry the skin with kitchen paper and bring the turkey to room temperature for 1 hour before cooking. Preheat the air fryer to 180°C for 3 minutes.

For the butter, put all the ingredients in a small bowl with ½ teaspoon salt and ¼ teaspoon pepper and beat for 2 minutes until smooth and creamy. Rub the butter under the turkey skin: you will have to get your fingers in, to loosen the skin carefully from the meat and ensure the butter also gets into the middle, without tearing the skin.

Place the onion rounds in a layer in the air fryer drawer, then set the turkey on top. Cook for 20 minutes. Reduce the air fryer temperature to 160°C and cook for a further 40 minutes. Remove the turkey and place on a plate or tray, wrap it tightly with foil and allow to rest for 15 minutes.

Meanwhile, to make the gravy, transfer the onion and juices from the air fryer to a saucepan. Add the butter and place over a medium heat. Using a wooden spoon, stir in the flour and cook for 2 minutes. Pour in the wine and stir well, scraping all the bits from the bottom of the pan. Allow to bubble for 2 minutes. Pour in the stock and allow to bubble for 5 minutes. Strain into another pan through a sieve, discarding the solids. Reduce the heat and simmer for 10 minutes, then season with salt and pepper.

Slice your turkey breast and serve immediately with the gravy.

MY NONNA ASSUNTA'S PORK RIBS WITH POTATOES AND ROSEMARY

Costine di maiale con patate e rosmarino di Nonna Assunta

SERVES 4

900g red skin potatoes, or
    Maris Piper potatoes, peeled
    and cut into chunks
1½ tablespoons olive oil
Leaves from 2 rosemary sprigs
1kg pork ribs, at room
    temperature
2 garlic cloves, unpeeled but
    roughly bashed
Salt and freshly ground
    black pepper

This is my father Ciro's favourite pork rib dish. His mother Assunta used to cook it for him in exactly the same way I am showing you; she didn't have an air fryer, of course, and she used to cook it in a wood-fired oven, but the ingredients and method are the same. Make it as spicy as you like by simply adding chilli flakes or powder to the marinade. You can substitute the pork ribs with chicken drumsticks or wings, if you prefer.

Preheat the air fryer to 180°C for 3 minutes.

Place the potato chunks in the air fryer fitted with the basket insert and toss them with half the oil, the rosemary, ½ teaspoon salt and ¼ teaspoon pepper. Cook for 20 minutes.

Meanwhile, cut each rack of pork ribs into 2 pieces and rub all over with the remaining oil, ½ teaspoon salt and ¼ teaspoon pepper.

Add the garlic to the potatoes, shake to toss well, then place the pork ribs on top. Cook for 20 minutes.

Turn over the ribs and continue to cook for a further 15 minutes. Plate up and serve with a nice cold beer or glass of wine.

GOLDEN CROQUETTES WITH MOZZARELLA AND HAM

Crocchette di patate con mozzarella filante e prosciutto cotto

MAKES 8

4 medium-sized Maris Piper
  potatoes or similar, scrubbed
40g finely grated Parmesan
  cheese
60g mozzarella cucina, cut into
  8 even-sized log shapes
50g cooked ham, cut into
  8 pieces
Salt and freshly ground
  black pepper

For the coating
80g panko breadcrumbs
1 tablespoon extra virgin
  olive oil
1 large egg, lightly beaten

These golden delights seriously take me back in time. My Nonno Giovanni, who was also a chef and remains my inspiration, used to make these for us all the time when we were kids. They are just insane and I've never met anyone that doesn't love them. They are fantastic for party nibbles and you can easily make them vegetarian by eliminating the ham or substituting it with semi-dried tomatoes. Honestly, please give them a try; they work so brilliantly with any meat or fish main course.

Pour 1.2 litres water into a large saucepan, add the potatoes and 1 teaspoon salt and bring to the boil. Cook for about 25 minutes until tender, then drain. Once cool enough to handle, peel, then put the flesh in a bowl and mash with the Parmesan cheese, ½ teaspoon salt and ¼ teaspoon pepper.

Wrap each log of mozzarella in a piece of ham.

Take a spoonful of potato mixture (about 50g) and compact it into a short oval shape about 8.5cm long; if your hands are slightly wet, it makes the mixture stick to your hands less. Make a dimple in the middle with your fingers and insert a ham-wrapped log of mozzarella. Seal with the potato mixture, giving it the classic cylinder shape of croquettes. Place on a plate, then repeat to form and stuff the remaining mixture. Chill them for 10 minutes.

Put the breadcrumbs in a bowl, add the extra virgin olive oil and mix using your fingertips as you would when making a crumble. Put the egg in a separate bowl. One at a time, dip the potato croquettes in the breadcrumbs, rolling them gently until all the surface is lightly covered. Gently transfer them to the bowl with the beaten egg, coat, letting any excess drip off, then again dip them back in the breadcrumbs, lightly pressing them into any gaps, coating the croquettes completely.

Preheat the air fryer to 190°C for 3 minutes.

Place the croquettes in the air fryer fitted with the basket insert and cook for 8 minutes. Carefully turn them and cook for a further 7 minutes. Let them stand for 5 minutes, then serve them hot.

ROASTED PUMPKIN LASAGNE

Lasagne di zucca arrostita con besciamella cremosa

SERVES 4

1kg pumpkin, cut into
  3cm slices
1 tablespoon olive oil
2 teaspoons chilli oil, or to taste
6 fresh lasagne sheets, each
  about 16 × 11cm
100g sliced speck ham
30g pine nuts
Salt and freshly ground
  black pepper

For the béchamel

70g salted butter, plus 20g cut
  into cubes
60g plain flour
700ml whole milk
70g finely grated Parmesan
  cheese
¼ small nutmeg, freshly grated

I hate waste and so I created this recipe after making pumpkin lanterns with my daughter Mia during Halloween one year. Sweet pumpkin works really well with the salty speck, the Parmesan and the kick of the chilli. This is a really fantastic, tasty lasagne which can easily become vegetarian by removing the speck. You can substitute Parmesan with pecorino cheese, speck with Parma ham, pine nuts with chopped blanched hazelnuts and the pumpkin with butternut squash, if you prefer; it will still be delicious.

Preheat the air fryer to 180°C for 3 minutes.

Place the pumpkin, olive oil, ¼ teaspoon salt and ¼ teaspoon pepper in the air fryer fitted with the basket insert and toss well. Cook for 20 minutes until just tender.

Meanwhile, make the béchamel by melting the 70g butter in a saucepan over a medium heat. Using a whisk, stir in the flour and cook for 1 minute until it is a light brown colour. Gradually stir in the milk, reduce the heat to low and cook for 8 minutes, stirring continuously. Once thickened, remove from the heat and stir in 40g of the Parmesan and the nutmeg. Season with ½ teaspoon salt and ¼ teaspoon pepper, stir again and set aside to slightly cool, then adjust the seasoning and nutmeg to your taste.

Reduce the air fryer temperature to 150°C.

Spread one-third of the béchamel in a 21cm square baking dish, or directly into the air fryer drawer, if yours is the same size, then drizzle in 1 teaspoon chilli oil. Lay 2 lasagne sheets on top; you'll need to trim one and add the trimmed piece to the gap above the sheets. Add half the pumpkin in an even layer, then half the speck and 10g pine nuts. Repeat these layers, then finish with a final layer of pasta and the remaining one-third of béchamel on top. Reserve the remaining pine nuts.

Cook for 20 minutes.

Increase the air fryer temperature to 160°C. Sprinkle over the remaining Parmesan cheese, pine nuts and the 20g cubed butter, grind pepper over the top and cook for a final 20 minutes, until golden and cooked through. Let it rest for 5 minutes before serving.

MY HEALTHY HANGOVER BRUNCH

Patate arrosto con uova, timo e pancetta

SERVES 4

900g red skin potatoes, or
    Maris Piper potatoes, cut
    into chunks
2 tablespoons olive oil
Leaves from 2 thyme sprigs
4 eggs
8 cured pancetta slices
2 large handfuls of rocket
Salt and freshly ground
    black pepper

For me, this makes the ultimate breakfast/brunch after partying with my boys. It never ceases to do the job: carbs and protein, perfect for soaking up the damage. Make sure the potatoes are nice and fluffy inside before you crack in the eggs and please make sure the eggs are super-fresh. You can substitute the cured pancetta with cooked ham, or Parma ham if you prefer, and try to portion the finished dish out carefully, so you don't break the eggs. Or, even better, don't bother plating it up, instead put the whole thing in the middle of the table and just dig in together.

Preheat the air fryer to 180°C for 3 minutes.

Place the potato chunks in the air fryer fitted with the basket insert, or a baking dish that fits in the air fryer, and toss with the oil, thyme and a generous pinch each of salt and pepper. Set in the air fryer drawer and cook for 20 minutes, shaking to toss twice during that time, until golden and fluffy inside.

Using a tablespoon, create 4 pockets in the bed of potatoes and gently crack an egg into each pocket. Cook for 5–8 minutes, depending on how done you like your eggs.

To serve, gently spoon out 4 portions, making sure everyone gets an egg. Place 2 slices of cured pancetta on each serving and top with some rocket leaves. Yum!

ROAST LEG OF LAMB WITH ROSEMARY, FENNEL AND PEPPER

Coscia di agnello arrosto con rosmarino, finocchietto e pepe nero

SERVES 6

1 bone-in leg of lamb, about
   1.3kg, removed from the
   fridge 1 hour before cooking

For the marinade

2 teaspoons fennel seeds
30g salted butter, at room
   temperature
5 anchovy fillets in oil
2 long rosemary sprigs, cut into
   small sprigs about 3cm long
Salt and freshly crushed
   black pepper

For the aïoli potatoes

1.2kg baby potatoes
3 tablespoons mayonnaise
1 tablespoon crème fraîche
1 small garlic clove, crushed
2 tablespoons chopped flat
   leaf parsley leaves
Finely grated zest and juice
   of ½ lemon

To serve

50g rocket or watercress
   leaves
1 tablespoon olive oil
Juice of ½ lemon

Here comes spring… this is one of my favourite roast meats and I always eat it with mint sauce, something we don't do in Italy but which I must admit works soooo well. Don't be put off by the anchovies, as the sweet lamb works perfectly with the salty little fish. You can substitute rosemary with thyme and crème fraîche with double cream or natural yogurt, if you prefer. Cooking the meat in an air fryer leaves you time to make all the other trimmings for your perfect Sunday roast. This is great with my Roasted peppers with parsley, garlic and extra virgin olive oil (see page 49).

Preheat the air fryer to 210°C for 3 minutes.

First, make the marinade. Roughly crush the fennel seeds in a mortar and pestle, then tip into a small bowl and mix with the butter, anchovies, ½ teaspoon salt and 1 teaspoon pepper. Mix well with a spoon until smooth and the anchovies are broken down. Cut slashes in the lamb about 1cm deep, then rub in the marinade all over, going into the slashes, too. Stick the rosemary sprigs all over the lamb in the slashes.

Place the lamb directly in the air fryer drawer and cook for 30 minutes until browned.

Reduce the air fryer temperature to 150°C and cook the lamb for a further 20 minutes.

Meanwhile, pour 3 litres water in a large saucepan with 1 tablespoon salt and bring to the boil. Add the potatoes and cook for 15 minutes or until tender, then drain in a colander and leave to dry. While they're still warm, tip them back into the cooled pan, add the mayo and crème fraîche, ¼ teaspoon pepper and ½ teaspoon salt, the garlic, parsley, lemon zest and juice. Mix gently but well with a wooden spoon.

Once the lamb is cooked, transfer to a plate and set aside to rest for 15 minutes, covered with foil.

Put the rocket or watercress leaves on a platter and dress with the olive oil, lemon juice and ¼ teaspoon each of salt and pepper. Mix well.

Place the lamb on top of the leaves, carve and place in the middle of the table along with the potatoes, for everyone to dig in.

BUTTER AND BAY LEAF HASSELBACK POTATOES

Ventagli di patate al forno con burro e alloro

SERVES 4

900g even-sized floury
   potatoes, such as Maris
   Piper, scrubbed (about
   90g each)
70g salted butter, cubed
1 tablespoon olive oil
5 bay leaves
8 thyme sprigs
Salt and freshly ground
   black pepper

These are my son Luciano's favourite potatoes. They look so fantastic and can be served with any meat or fish, especially when entertaining, but the D'Acampos have even been known to eat them for breakfast with my special Sunday fry-up and they always get a 'Hell, yeah!' when served. They are such a great alternative to regular roast potatoes. You can make them spicy by adding a little chilli oil on top if you like, and you can substitute the thyme with rosemary.

Pour 2.5 litres water and 1 tablespoon salt into a large saucepan and bring to the boil. Once it gets to a fast boil, add the potatoes and cook them for 16 minutes until almost tender. You want them to hold their shape, so be careful not to overcook. Drain and leave in the colander to dry for 5 minutes.

Melt the butter in small bowl in the microwave, add the oil, ½ teaspoon salt and ¼ teaspoon pepper and mix well.

Preheat the air fryer to 180°C for 3 minutes.

One at a time, place a potato on a chopping board and lay wooden spoons or chopsticks along both of the long sides. Use a sharp knife to cut the potato across into about 5mm slices, stopping when your knife reaches the spoons or chopsticks so the potato stays intact at the bottom. Repeat the process with the rest of the potatoes.

Place the potatoes sliced side up in a 19cm pie dish or cake tin. Brush two-thirds of the seasoned butter generously over the potatoes, then slot the herbs in the cuts at random.

Cook for 15 minutes, then remove, brush the remaining butter over and continue to cook for a further 15 minutes until golden. Serve immediately.

Those of you who know my style will know that I'm not a fan of fussy food. I love using fresh, simple ingredients and allowing them to shine, and, in this chapter, I really believe I prove that. These recipes just scream of a true Mediterranean diet, in which seasonal fruit and vegetables, herbs and pulses are hugely important, though fish and meat feature prominently too. Italians would tend to simply grill a piece of fish or meat and serve it with a light lemon dressing, say, rather than a heavy cream sauce.

It might be because of the climate, maybe in Italy specifically, but everyone chooses to buy and eat local produce, the ingredients are super-fresh and somehow what you cook feels more like clean eating. In Italy, I love going to the markets and picking the best vegetables on offer, touching and sniffing them, rather than just being faced with impenetrable plastic packaging.

The Italian diet is one of the healthiest cuisines, with many people living to a ripe old age. That just goes to prove that a little pizza, pasta and wine – not to mention fresh fish, vegetables and pulses – are essential to us. I have counted the calories of each portion of food made in the recipes in this chapter to prove that tasty Italian food can still be easy on our hips.

My salmon and olive recipe in this chapter is a must-try and the dish works well with any white fish, too. Olives and tomatoes mean summer freshness to me, so I hope it brings a little bit of Italy to you at home. You might be surprised to see a bucatini recipe here, as this shape of pasta is quite heavy in texture, but it really does complement aubergines perfectly. Another dish I'd really like you to try is the polenta-crusted chicken. The lightness of polenta mixed with herbs gives the chicken a fantastic crispness and flavour, adding that little something extra, instead of being just coated in regular breadcrumbs. I really hope, with every bite, you enjoy these recipes as much as I do and that they transport you back to some fabulous memories... hopefully from wonderful days in Italy!

THE
MED
DIET

MEDITERRANEAN-STYLE SALMON WITH OLIVES AND CHERRY TOMATOES

Salmone alla Mediterranea con olive e pomodorini

SERVES 4

600g baby potatoes, halved
    if larger
2 tablespoons extra virgin
    olive oil
1 teaspoon dried oregano
250g red and yellow cherry
    tomatoes
1 garlic clove, crushed
60g pitted Taggiasca olives
1 tablespoon capers in
    vinegar, drained
4 skinless salmon fillets, about
    110g each
Finely grated zest and juice of
    ½ large lemon
10 basil leaves
Salt and freshly ground
    black pepper

470 KCAL *for each portion*

The colours of this dish alone make me happy, it's just so pretty. Don't only judge its looks though, because it's also a fantastic recipe that gives you everything you need: fish, carbs and vegetables. I love making this for my family when we are home in Sardinia. It's light on those hot days, filling on the cold days and just so tasty. You can substitute the salmon with cod or any other firm white fish fillets, if you prefer.

Preheat the air fryer to 180°C for 3 minutes.

Place the potatoes in a round ovenproof dish about 20cm in diameter and toss with half the oil, half the oregano, ½ teaspoon salt and ½ teaspoon pepper. Cook for 20 minutes until the potatoes are tender, shaking to toss once halfway through.

Meanwhile, in a small bowl, mix the remaining oil and oregano, the cherry tomatoes, garlic, olives and capers, season with ½ teaspoon salt and ½ teaspoon pepper and mix well.

Place the salmon fillets on top of the potatoes, tip over the tomato mixture and bake for 10–12 minutes.

To serve, add the lemon zest and juice and sprinkle over the basil.

SPAGHETTI FRITTATA WITH COURGETTES AND PECORINO ROMANO

Frittata di spaghetti con zucchine e pecorino Romano

SERVES 2

2 small courgettes, total
   weight about 300g, cut
   into 2cm slices
2½ teaspoons olive oil
100g dried spaghetti
4 eggs
1 tablespoon chopped flat leaf
   parsley leaves
40g pecorino Romano cheese,
   finely grated
75g frozen peas, defrosted
Salt and freshly ground
   black pepper

465 KCAL *for each portion*

A classic Neapolitan way of using leftover spaghetti, or linguine, or indeed any similar long pasta. This is a very versatile recipe to which you can add or remove pretty much whatever you fancy, except for the eggs and pasta! Any grated cheese will do instead of the pecorino Romano and you can substitute parsley with chopped chives if you prefer. I have also added 80g chopped cooked ham to the frittata mixture before, which tastes fantastic.

Preheat the air fryer to 180°C for 3 minutes.

Place the courgettes in the air fryer fitted with the basket insert, toss with 2 teaspoons oil and ½ teaspoon salt and cook for 5 minutes. Shake to toss the courgette slices, then cook for a further 5 minutes until golden. Set aside.

Meanwhile, in a saucepan, bring 1.5 litres water to the boil with 1 teaspoon salt. Add the pasta and cook for 2 minutes less than instructed on the packet for the perfect al dente bite, stirring every now and then with a wooden spoon. Drain.

Oil a 20cm ovenproof dish (mine had a 15cm base) with the remaining oil. As long as the dish fits in your air fryer, it will be fine.

Reduce the air fryer temperature to 150°C.

Crack the eggs into a large bowl, and, with a whisk, beat in the parsley, ⅛ teaspoon salt, ¼ teaspoon black pepper and half the cheese until smooth. Add half the peas, half the courgette slices and the cooked pasta and mix well using a wooden spoon. Pour into your prepared dish, spreading it out to evenly cover.

Scatter over the remaining courgette slices and peas, sprinkle the remaining pecorino cheese on top and cook for 15–20 minutes until cooked through. (It will cook much more quickly in a metal dish than in a silicone container.) Serve immediately.

BUCATINI WITH AUBERGINE, TOMATOES AND TOASTED ALMONDS

Bucatini con salsa di melanzane, pomodori freschi e mandorle tostate

SERVES 4

50g blanched almonds
550g mixed tomatoes, big
    tomatoes cut into 4cm
    chunks, cherry tomatoes
    kept whole
30ml extra virgin olive oil, plus
    4 teaspoons
1 small garlic clove, finely
    chopped
1 aubergine (about 300g),
    cut into 3cm cubes
320g dried bucatini pasta
60g finely grated pecorino
    Romano cheese, plus 20g
    to serve
10 basil leaves
Salt and freshly ground
    black pepper

581 KCAL *for each portion*

This is the kind of recipe I love to cook in the summer in Sardinia, when the tomatoes are bursting with flavour and the aubergines are at their best. I'm super-lucky as I grow them there myself and there is nothing quite like picking home-grown vegetables to create a delicious summer sauce. If you have time, make the sauce the day before, as it will taste even better after a night in the fridge. You can actually just serve the sauce as it is, in my opinion, but with pasta it's amazing (you can substitute the bucatini with any long, or large-tube, pasta). A little chilli oil is also nice, if you fancy a kick.

Preheat the air fryer to 180°C for 3 minutes.

Toast the almonds in the air fryer for 6 minutes. Once cool enough to handle, finely chop, then set aside.

In a small bowl, place all the tomatoes and add 2 teaspoons extra virgin olive oil, the garlic, ½ teaspoon salt and ¼ teaspoon pepper and gently mix. Using 2 sheets of foil for added strength, gather the foil to create a little bowl, tip in the tomatoes and seal to encase completely.

Peel strips of skin off the aubergine, so it is striped black and white, then cut it into 2cm cubes. Toss the aubergine with 2 teaspoons extra virgin olive oil and ½ teaspoon salt, then cook in the air fryer fitted with the basket insert for 13 minutes. Shake to toss the aubergine, then move it to one side of the basket insert. Place the foil-wrapped tomatoes in the space you created and cook for a further 12 minutes.

Meanwhile, pour 4 litres water into a large saucepan, add 1 tablespoon salt and bring to the boil. Add the pasta and cook for 1 minute less than instructed by the packet for that perfect al dente bite, stirring occasionally with a wooden spoon. Drain.

In the same hot saucepan, tip in the cooked aubergine, tomatoes and their juices from the foil, the 30ml extra virgin olive oil, the almonds, the 60g pecorino cheese and the basil, mix well using a wooden spoon, roughly breaking up the tomatoes as you go, then season to taste.

Toss in the cooked pasta, ensuring it is well coated in the sauce, sprinkle over the remaining pecorino, then serve immediately.

CHICKEN LEGS WITH POTATOES, LEMONS AND CAPERS

Cosce di pollo con patate al limone e capperi

SERVES 4

900g red skin potatoes,
    or Maris Piper potatoes,
    scrubbed and cut into
    3cm chunks
2 teaspoons olive oil
6 sage leaves
40g salted butter, at room
    temperature
4 chicken legs, total weight
    about 900g, at room
    temperature
2 tablespoons nonpareil
    capers, plus 1 tablespoon
    caper brine
Finely grated zest of 1 lemon,
    and juice of 2 lemons (about
    4 tablespoons)
1 tablespoon finely chopped
    flat leaf parsley leaves
Salt and freshly ground
    black pepper

499 KCAL *for each portion*

A super-easy, fresh-flavoured and tasty recipe. You can replace the chicken legs with small pork ribs or chicken wings, if you prefer, or even a combination of all of them. I have used Leccino pitted olives instead of capers before, which is lovely, but capers are such a great flavour. The origins and the use of capers date back to very ancient times; in fact, they are even mentioned by ancient Roman writers such as Pliny, so we have to give them the respect they deserve and not save them only to serve with fish.

Preheat the air fryer to 180°C for 3 minutes.

Place the potatoes in the air fryer fitted with the basket insert and toss with the oil, sage, ½ teaspoon salt and ¼ teaspoon pepper. Cook for 20 minutes.

Meanwhile, rub the butter all over the chicken skin and season with ½ teaspoon salt and ¼ teaspoon pepper. Shake to toss the potatoes, then place the chicken legs on top. Cook for 20 minutes, then turn the chicken and cook for a further 10 minutes until golden and cooked through. Sprinkle over the drained capers and cook for 5 minutes so they crisp up.

To serve, plate up the chicken and potatoes, then tip the capers that are still in the basket insert into the air fryer drawer. Add the caper brine, lemon zest and juice, mix well with the buttery juices in the drawer, then finally add the parsley and a pinch of salt and pepper to taste. Mix well and spoon over the chicken.

Serve with a crisp green salad and nice cold beer or glass of white wine.

LAMB KEBABS

Spiedini di agnello marinato con aglio, peperoni e cipolla rossa

SERVES 4

150g natural yogurt
1 tablespoon extra virgin
    olive oil
1 tablespoon lemon juice
¾ teaspoon dried mint
1 garlic clove, crushed
2 tablespoons finely chopped
    rosemary leaves
600g lamb, cut into 4cm
    pieces (leg is good)
2 red or orange peppers,
    about 210g each, cut into
    3cm chunks
2 small red onions, each cut
    into 8 wedges
Salt and freshly ground
    black pepper
Sea salt flakes, to serve

457 KCAL *for each portion*

This is a great recipe for a barbecue, but, as it can also be cooked in an air fryer, that gives us the luxury of being able to eat it all year round. Lamb is at its best eaten hot, so making the dish in two batches ensures the next skewer is ready to serve once the first is finished. You can make them spicy by simply adding 1 teaspoon chilli powder to the marinade and I also like to add a courgette wheel to the skewers sometimes. My air fryer has a top temperature of 230°C, so, while it browns the outside of the skewers, the meat cooks slowly inside and stays tender. You can substitute the lamb with chicken chunks, if you prefer.

Place eight 18cm wooden skewers in a in small, shallow dish filled with water, so they are covered completely. Leave to soak for 10 minutes. (This stops them from burning in the air fryer.)

Pour the yogurt into a bowl with the oil, lemon juice, mint, garlic and rosemary. Season with ½ teaspoon salt and ½ teaspoon pepper. Add the lamb and mix well, coating each piece with the marinade. Leave to rest at room temperature for 10 minutes.

Preheat the air fryer to 230°C for 3 minutes.

Take the skewers out of the water, then thread 3 pieces of lamb on to each skewer, alternating each piece with chunks of pepper and wedges of onion.

Working in 2 batches, place 4 skewers in the air fryer fitted with the basket insert, evenly spaced, 3 in a row and 1 at the top. Cook for 10 minutes.

Sprinkle over some sea salt flakes and enjoy, while you cook the second batch of skewers. I like to serve these with a crispy salad, or my Super-crispy polenta chips (see page 165) and a dish of minted yogurt, if you like, for dipping.

AUNTY CLARA'S STUFFED AUBERGINES WITH LENTILS AND MOZZARELLA

Melanzane ripiene di zia Clara con lenticchie e mozzarella

SERVES 4

2 large aubergines, about
    350g each
5 tablespoons olive oil
1 small onion, chopped
1 small red pepper, chopped
400g can of chopped
    tomatoes
400g can of brown lentils,
    drained and rinsed
½ teaspoon dried oregano, or
    the leaves from 2 thyme or
    oregano sprigs
¼ teaspoon chilli flakes,
    or Calabrian chilli paste
    from a jar
10 basil leaves, half chopped,
    half left whole
125g mozzarella ball, drained
    and torn
Salt and freshly ground
    black pepper

408 KCAL *for each portion*

Whether you are vegetarian or not, you won't be disappointed when this is served up; you will absolutely not miss fish or meat. Once you have mastered the recipe, you can be as creative as you like with the filling. You can substitute the lentils with canned cannellini beans and the mozzarella with a strong grated Cheddar cheese or goat's cheese, if you prefer. Honestly anything goes. I really hope I made my Aunty Clara proud with this creation.

Preheat the air fryer to 170°C for 3 minutes.

Cut the aubergines in half lengthways. Score the flesh with a sharp knife, making shallow criss-cross cuts in the flesh. Rub in 4 tablespoons olive oil, sprinkle over a generous pinch each of salt and pepper, then place in the air fryer fitted with the basket insert (they will overlap now, but they will shrink). Cook for 20 minutes.

Meanwhile, in a saucepan, fry the onion and pepper in the remaining olive oil for 5 minutes over a medium heat, until softened and lightly golden. Add the tomatoes, lentils, oregano and chilli. Bring to the boil, then simmer gently for 10 minutes, stirring occasionally.

Once the aubergines are cooked, remove from the air fryer and use a spoon to scoop out the flesh from the centre of the aubergines. Roughly chop the aubergine flesh and add to the tomato sauce, with the chopped basil, ½ teaspoon salt and ½ teaspoon pepper. Stir well to combine.

Spoon the tomato mixture evenly between each aubergine skin. Top with the mozzarella. Place back in the air fryer and cook for a further 8–10 minutes until golden. Sprinkle over the basil leaves and serve.

POLENTA-CRUSTED CHICKEN BREASTS WITH CHILLI AND LEMON ZEST

Petti di pollo in crosta di polenta al peperoncino e limone

SERVES 4

60g fine polenta
1 small garlic clove, crushed
1 tablespoon finely chopped
  flat leaf parsley leaves
1 tablespoon finely chopped
  sage leaves, or 1 teaspoon
  dried sage
½ teaspoon chilli flakes, or
  1 teaspoon if you want
  it spicy
Finely grated zest of 1 lemon,
  plus lemon wedges to serve
30g finely grated Parmesan
  cheese
4 skinless chicken breasts, each
  about 150g
1½ tablespoons olive oil
Salt and freshly ground
  black pepper

292 KCAL *for each portion*

In this recipe I've used polenta, which gives the chicken a lovely crust, but of course dried breadcrumbs can also be used if you prefer (and will only add about five calories to each portion). Try to buy even-sized 150g chicken breasts if you can, as smaller pieces will cook more quickly and so won't have time to crisp up as much. I ran out of lemons once and used orange zest to make these instead, which was also lovely if you fancy something different. You can serve this dish with any carb, seasonal green or salad, but I've suggested My healthy hangover brunch (see page 120), purely because I was out last night and that's what I fancied...

In a tray, mix the polenta, garlic, parsley, sage, chilli, lemon zest, Parmesan, ½ teaspoon salt and ¼ teaspoon pepper until well combined.

On a plate, rub each chicken breast all over with olive oil. One at a time, press the chicken gently into the polenta mixture, turn and press again to completely cover for an even crust.

Preheat the air fryer to 190°C for 3 minutes.

Set the coated chicken in the air fryer fitted with the basket insert and cook for 12 minutes, until golden and cooked through. Serve immediately with lemon wedges.

SPICY GLAZED PORK CHOPS WITH HOT HONEY AND SLAW

Costolette di maiale glassate con 'nduja e miele

SERVES 4

2–4 teaspoons Calabrian chilli paste from a jar (to taste, it's very spicy), or 50g 'nduja from a jar
5 teaspoons runny honey
2 teaspoons balsamic glaze
2 teaspoons thyme leaves
1 tablespoon olive oil
4 pork chops, about 200g each, at room temperature
Salt and freshly ground black pepper

For the slaw
½ small white cabbage
½ red onion
1 small fennel bulb
30g mayonnaise
60g crème fraîche, or natural yogurt
1 tablespoon white wine vinegar
2 tablespoons chopped chives

563 KCAL for each portion, or **621 KCAL** if using 'nduja

Some of you may glance at the ingredients here and not be familiar with Calabrian chilli paste or 'nduja. I use it in a quite few recipes when I want the food to give a kick. They are both definitely great store cupboard staples and give a lot of flavour for these quick recipes. You'll find them in jars in most larger supermarkets. The sweet and spicy glaze I created is perfect with chops, but works equally well with pork ribs or chicken drumsticks. Try these with my Golden croquettes with mozzarella and ham (see page 116).

First, make the marinade by mixing the chilli paste or 'nduja, honey, balsamic glaze, thyme and oil in a wide, shallow bowl until smooth. Cut a few very light slashes in the pork on both sides, to help the marinade penetrate. Rub the pork with ½ teaspoon salt and ¼ teaspoon pepper, then toss and coat in the marinade. Leave for 30 minutes for the flavours to infuse.

Meanwhile, trim and very finely slice or shred the cabbage, onion and fennel. Place in a bowl and mix in the mayonnaise, crème fraîche or yogurt, vinegar, ½ teaspoon salt and ½ teaspoon pepper. Mix well and taste for seasoning. Fold in the chives, cover with clingfilm and refrigerate until needed.

Preheat the air fryer to 180°C for 3 minutes.

Set the pork in the air fryer fitted with the basket insert, spacing the chops out evenly. Bake for 10 minutes, or up to 16 minutes, depending how thick the chops are, until cooked through.

Plate up with your slaw.

All these dishes are simply recipes for two and I have chosen a real variety, to cater for all the important people in my life. I have often made them for my best friend Marco when he comes over, or even just for my boys, and they all love the steaks with creamy spinach or the lamb chops. If I'm doing dinner for two for my little princess, Mia would always choose the wrapped baked sea bream. My wife Jessica would choose asparagus and Gorgonzola tart or chicken Kyiv, while my in-laws love the pistachio and Parma ham lasagne. The family enjoy so many of these that we often double up the quantities and eat them as a family meal.

Date night can be fun at home (for obvious reasons!) but sitting down chatting, enjoying a glass of wine and cooking together is just a perfect night, in my opinion. What's fantastic about using an air fryer is that you really can be free to do... whatever you like, while your delicious meal is cooking. Making dinner for the family can be a bit lonely sometimes, especially when – as so often happens – they only all arrive when the food is ready, but cooking for two can be much more fun, romantic and just so enjoyable. If you are cooking for a partner for the first time, I suggest you make the chicken in creamy saffron lemon sauce. It's super-tasty, looks really impressive and is light enough for you to partake in any other activity you may have planned...

I also recommend you take a look at the Sweet chapter. Everyone loves a cheeky dessert on date night, even me, who usually opts for fruit after a meal. I hope these recipes leave you and your guest culinarily satisfied, then the rest is up to you... Good luck x

WHOLE SEA BREAM WITH LEMON AND PROSECCO, WITH FENNEL SALAD

Orata intera con limone, prosecco e finocchio

SERVES 2

2 large lemons
1 whole sea bream, about
   800g, scaled and gutted
   (wink at your fishmonger and
   ask them to do it for you)
50g salted butter, very soft
2 tablespoons prosecco
1 tablespoon capers in brine,
   drained
Salt and freshly ground
   black pepper

For the salad
½ fennel bulb
1 tablespoon olive oil
40g rocket
1 tablespoon chopped flat leaf
   parsley leaves

The lemon and butter here cook down to make a delicious sauce with the tart capers. My wife isn't a fish lover, so rarely cooks fish at home. She often says she's worried about getting it wrong, but even she says this is a super-easy recipe, including if you have never cooked fish before. You can substitute the sea bream with sea bass, if you prefer. The recipe has you opening a bottle of prosecco and only using a couple of tablespoons: obviously that's the perfect excuse to serve the fish with a cold glass of prosecco or two!

Zest and juice one of the lemons and cut the other into 4 slices, reserving its ends for squeezing over the fennel later.

Cut a sheet each of baking paper and foil big enough to wrap the fish. Place the fish on the baking paper with the foil underneath. Put the lemon slices in the cavity, then season the fish inside and out with ½ teaspoon salt and ¼ teaspoon pepper.

Preheat the air fryer to 190°C for 3 minutes.

Gather the foil and baking paper to create a kind of bowl, with the top open and the fish in the centre. Rub the skin with about half the butter, then cut the remaining butter into cubes or chunks and place it in the paper with the fish. Now set the fish and its foil/baking paper bowl in the air fryer fitted with the basket insert (you'll have to wrap the tail around a little to make it fit). Pour the prosecco into the cavity of the fish, then scatter the capers and lemon zest on top and pour in the lemon juice. Cook for 20 minutes, or until cooked through.

Meanwhile, finely slice the fennel, put it into a bowl, squeeze the ends of the sliced lemon over it immediately and toss to coat, to stop it from turning brown, then toss in the oil, rocket and parsley. Season with 1 teaspoon salt and ¼ teaspoon pepper and mix with a metal spoon.

Remove the fish from the air fryer and place on a serving plate, still in the foil and paper. Spoon over the buttery juices and serve with the salad.

BRUSCHETTA WITH MARINATED TOMATOES AND CREAMY BURRATA

Bruschetta con pomodori marinati e burrata

SERVES 2 / MAKES 4

For the topping

300g mixed tomatoes, large
  tomatoes roughly chopped,
  cherry tomatoes left whole
Pinch of chilli flakes
2 teaspoons extra virgin olive
  oil, plus more to serve
8 basil leaves, half torn, half
  left whole
1 burrata ball, about 200g
Sea salt flakes and freshly
  ground black pepper

For the bruschetta

4 teaspoons extra virgin
  olive oil
4 slices of ciabatta, about
  1cm thick
Pinch of dried oregano

I have to put some kind of bruschetta recipe into every book I write, not only because it's a traditional Italian must-have, but because it's so hugely popular all around the world. This particular version is the best-selling starter across all my restaurants. Burrata dates back to about 1900 and is a typical product of Puglia in the south of Italy. It is produced from cow's milk, rennet and cream and it is said that it was originally made by brothers Lorenzo and Vincenzo Bianchino on a farm in the town of Andria. For those who don't like or can't get burrata, you can also use buffalo mozzarella or ricotta.

Preheat the air fryer to 180°C for 3 minutes.

Take a large piece of foil and mould it like a bowl that will fit in your air fryer, leaving it open at the top.

Place all the tomatoes in a small bowl. Add ½ teaspoon salt, ¼ teaspoon pepper, chilli flakes and the 2 teaspoons extra virgin olive oil and gently stir to combine. Carefully pour into your foil bowl, leaving the top open, then air fry for 8 minutes. Add the torn basil leaves, gently stir and leave to marinate while you make the bruschetta.

Increase the air fryer temperature to 200°C and put in the basket insert.

Brush ½ teaspoon extra virgin olive oil over each slice of bread, along with a pinch of oregano, ¼ teaspoon salt and ¼ teaspoon pepper. Air fry for 3 minutes, then drizzle each with another ½ teaspoon olive oil and flip over for another 2 minutes. Divide the tomatoes equally between the bruschetta. Gently tear the burrata into pieces and divide evenly between each bruschetta with 1 basil leaf. Pour over a little more olive oil, season to taste and serve immediately.

CHICKEN KYIV WITH SAGE AND PECORINO ROMANO

Petto di pollo ripieno di burro alla salvia, aglio e pecorino Romano

SERVES 2

2 skinless chicken breasts, about 220g each
1 tablespoon olive oil, or olive oil spray

For the filling

2 garlic cloves, crushed
40g butter, at room temperature
⅛ nutmeg, finely grated
15g finely grated pecorino Romano cheese
½ tablespoon chopped flat leaf parsley leaves
½ tablespoon finely chopped sage leaves
Salt and freshly ground black pepper

For the coating

1 egg, lightly beaten
2 tablespoons plain flour
55g panko breadcrumbs
2½ teaspoons olive oil

A classic with an Italian twist, in which the salty pecorino Romano works beautifully with the sweet butter and sage. In my house, we cook this once a month and sometimes we add a slice of cooked ham with the flavoured butter. This is perfect if you have guests, as you can prepare the chicken in the morning – it's easy to scale up the recipe – and cook when people arrive. My Sliced courgettes with mint, garlic and white wine vinegar (see page 26) complement this dish amazingly well.

First, make the filling by mixing all the ingredients with ½ teaspoon salt and ¼ teaspoon pepper until smooth. Use a spatula to scrape into a log shape, then place on a small sheet of clingfilm. Use the clingfilm to help you roll it into a sausage, twist the ends so it's like a cracker, to seal and tighten the butter, then keep in the freezer while you prepare the chicken.

Place a chicken breast on a chopping board and put one hand flat on top of it, to keep it steady. Carefully slice horizontally into the middle of the breast with a sharp knife. You want to make a slit about 5cm long that reaches about three-quarters of the way through the breast, creating a pocket. Repeat for the other breast. Put the beaten egg in a small bowl.

Season the chicken with ½ teaspoon salt and ¼ teaspoon pepper. Slice the flavoured butter into 2 discs. Tuck a butter disc into each pocket and tuck the excess meat in, using some of the beaten egg to glue and seal any loose bits. Chill for 10 minutes.

Put the plain flour in a bowl and the breadcrumbs with the 2½ teaspoons oil in another, mixing the crumbs and oil together using your fingertips, as you would when making crumble. Have the beaten egg to hand, too.

One at a time, coat the chicken lightly in the flour. Now dip in the egg, letting any excess drip off. Finally coat in breadcrumbs, lightly pressing crumbs into any gaps and making sure all the pockets are sealed shut. If you have time, chill for another 30 minutes.

Preheat the air fryer to 170°C for 3 minutes.

Take the chicken from the fridge, place it in the air fryer fitted with the basket insert and cook for 30 minutes. Leave to stand for 3 minutes, then serve with crispy radicchio or rocket leaves, or salad of your choice.

ASPARAGUS, GORGONZOLA AND HONEY TART

Torta di asparagi, Gorgonzola e miele

SERVES 2

320g sheet of puff pastry
  (you'll use half)
1 egg
80g Gorgonzola cheese,
  crumbled
250g asparagus spears
1 teaspoon poppy seeds
4 teaspoons runny honey
Salt and freshly ground
  black pepper

Perfect for a light date night, this is quick to prepare, tasty and filling, but not too much, so you can enjoy the rest of the evening… If the Gorgonzola is too strong for you, try the recipe with Dolcelatte or goat's cheese instead. You can be as creative as you like with the toppings; in the past, I've made this with courgettes instead of asparagus, for example, or you can substitute the honey with maple syrup if you prefer. This is fantastic with a crispy salad and a cheeky cold glass of Italian dry white wine.

Unroll the puff pastry sheet with a long side closest to you. Trim a 3cm strip from the end (so it fits in your air fryer). Cut the remaining sheet in half to get two 19cm squares. Wrap and freeze the one of the squares along with the trimmings for another time. (You can use them to make my Almond and raspberry frangipane tart, see page 189.)

In a bowl, lightly beat the egg with ¼ teaspoon salt.

Preheat the air fryer to 180°C for 3 minutes.

Run a knife around the edge of the pastry to lightly score a 2cm border, then prick the pastry all over the middle section with a fork. Brush with some of the egg, carefully set in the air fryer fitted with the basket insert (so hot air can circulate under the pastry and make it super-crisp) and cook for 25 minutes.

Meanwhile, add the Gorgonzola and ¼ teaspoon pepper to the remaining egg and roughly mash together with a fork to make a chunky, loose paste. Snap or cut the ends off the asparagus: you'll feel a natural break; that's the woody ends coming off. Peel them if you prefer. If any spears are particularly thick, halve them lengthways.

Spoon the egg mixture into the middle section of the pastry, roughly spread to the edges of the border, then place the asparagus on top, spaced out evenly. Sprinkle over the poppy seeds and cook for another 10 minutes.

Remove the tart from the air fryer, then set on a serving plate with a spatula. Drizzle over the honey and serve.

CHICKEN SUPREMES WITH SAFFRON-LEMON SAUCE

Suprema di pollo con salsa di zafferano e limone

SERVES 2

2 chicken supremes, with skin,
about 250g each
20g salted butter, at room
temperature
Salt and freshly ground
black pepper

For the gremolata
3 tablespoons finely chopped
flat leaf parsley leaves
1 garlic clove, crushed
Finely grated zest of 1 lemon

For the sauce
Pinch of saffron threads (or
see recipe introduction)
2 egg yolks
½ teaspoon cornflour
150ml double cream
2 teaspoons lemon juice,
or to taste

This is a really great-tasting recipe which will impress your guest and won't take long to prepare, leaving you time to be with them. You can substitute saffron threads with saffron powder, if you prefer. You definitely should have some warm crusty bread to hand, to mop up the sauce, even if you decide to serve this with potatoes... the dunky-dunky of bread at the end is a must! The sauce here also works really well with fish. However you do it, make sure you serve it with a cold bottle of Italian dry white wine.

Preheat the air fryer to 180°C for 3 minutes.

Dry the chicken skin with kitchen paper, then rub the butter all over the skin. Sprinkle 2 pinches each of salt and pepper over each supreme, making sure you really cover the skin.

Place the chicken in the air fryer fitted with the basket insert and cook for 15 minutes.

Increase the air fryer temperature to 200°C and cook for a further 15 minutes, until the skin is golden and the chicken is cooked through.

Meanwhile, place all the ingredients for the gremolata in a small bowl and mix well. Set aside until needed.

For the sauce, put the saffron in a small bowl with 1 tablespoon warm water and leave to infuse for 5 minutes.

In a small saucepan, mix the egg yolks and cornflour using a whisk until smooth, pour in the cream and whisk again until combined. Place over a low heat. Simmer gently, stirring constantly with the whisk, for 3 minutes. Add the lemon juice and the saffron threads with their soaking water, ½ teaspoon salt and ¼ teaspoon pepper and stir with your whisk for a further 1–2 minutes until the sauce has thickened. Taste the sauce and add more lemon, salt and pepper as you prefer.

Divide the sauce equally between 2 warmed plates and gently place the chicken on top, skin side up. Sprinkle over the gremolata and serve immediately with a crispy green salad, or my Roasted peppers with parsley, garlic and extra virgin olive oil (see page 49).

LASAGNE WITH PISTACHIOS, PARMA HAM AND MOZZARELLA

Lasagne con pistacchi, prosciutto crudo e mozzarella

SERVES 2

4 fresh egg lasagne sheets,
    each about 16 × 11cm
100g Parma ham
40g pistachio nuts, shelled
    and chopped
200g buffalo mozzarella ball,
    drained and torn

For the béchamel
40g salted butter, plus 10g
    cut into cubes
30g plain flour
500ml whole milk
1/8 small nutmeg, freshly grated,
    plus more to taste
25g finely grated Parmesan
    cheese
Salt and freshly ground
    black pepper

Lasagne with a difference: a must-try. This version is very easy and just as tasty as the classic, but eliminates the process of cooking the Bolognese sauce, so it's ready in less than an hour. It's a perfect dish for a romantic Sunday dinner for two, with a bottle of Italian full-bodied red wine. For best results, use fresh egg lasagne sheets, as the richness of the egg pasta really does enhance the flavours. You can substitute mozzarella for a good-quality grated Cheddar cheese and the Parma ham with sliced cooked ham, if you prefer.

To prepare the béchamel, place a saucepan over a medium heat and melt the 40g butter. Using a whisk, stir in the flour and cook for 1 minute until it becomes light brown. Gradually whisk in the milk, reduce the heat to low and cook for 8 minutes, stirring constantly. Once it has thickened, stir in the nutmeg, 1/3 teaspoon salt, 1/4 teaspoon pepper and half the Parmesan. Remove from the heat and set aside to cool slightly. Taste and adjust the seasoning and nutmeg to your preference.

Preheat the air fryer to 150°C for 3 minutes.

Spread one-quarter of the béchamel in an ovenproof dish (about 20 × 13 × 6cm), then lay a lasagne sheet on top. Add one-third of the Parma ham and sprinkle over one-quarter of the pistachios. Place one-quarter of the mozzarella cheese on top. Repeat these layers 2 more times, finishing with the last lasagne sheet and remaining béchamel on top. Keep the remaining mozzarella and pistachios aside for now. Cover with foil and seal tightly around the sides, but be sure the foil 'tents' the lasagne so it doesn't touch the surface. Place the lasagne in the air fryer and cook for 20 minutes.

Increase the air fryer temperature to 160°C.

Remove the foil and evenly sprinkle over the remaining Parmesan cheese and pistachios. Place on the remaining mozzarella, well spaced out, and dot over the 10g cubed butter. Grind some black pepper all over and cook for 15 minutes until golden and cooked through. Remove and let rest for 5 minutes before serving.

LAMB CHOPS WITH CRISPY PANCETTA, PEAS AND HONEY

Costolette di agnello con pancetta, piselli e miele

SERVES 2

2 large or 4 small lamb chops,
  at room temperature
1 teaspoon extra virgin olive oil
125g smoked pancetta lardons
150g frozen peas, defrosted
½ tablespoon honey
2 pinches of dried oregano
1 tablespoon chopped
  mint leaves
1 spring onion, finely sliced
Finely grated zest and juice of
  ½ large lemon
Salt and freshly ground
  black pepper

I am a huge advocate of using seasonal vegetables and lamb when in season, but I must admit that a cheeky lamb chop at any time of the year is OK in my book (literally). I just love its flavour. You can substitute pancetta with guanciale (cured pork cheek) if you prefer, or the flavours in this recipe also work well with a pork chop. Please make sure the chops are at room temperature before starting the recipe. I cooked 2 large chops that weighed about 200g each, but if you have slightly thicker or smaller chops, the cooking time will increase or reduce respectively by a couple of minutes.

Preheat the air fryer to 215°C for 3 minutes.

Season the lamb chops with salt and pepper and rub with the olive oil. Cook the chops for 7 minutes in the air fryer fitted with the basket insert. Turn the chops over, add the pancetta around them and cook for 4 minutes more, then tip in the peas and cook for a further 4 minutes.

Take out the chops, place on a plate and cover with foil. Spoon the peas and pancetta into a bowl, leaving the fat behind. Drizzle the honey into the peas and pancetta with the herbs, spring onion and lemon zest and juice, then mix well and serve with the lamb.

SUPER-CRISPY POLENTA CHIPS WITH SALSA TONNATA

Tranci di polenta croccante con salsa tonnata

SERVES 2

125g quick-cook polenta
20g salted butter, cut into cubes
1 tablespoon finely chopped rosemary leaves
1 tablespoon olive oil
Salt and freshly ground black pepper

For the sauce

320g tuna chunks in olive oil, from a can or in a jar, drained (see recipe introduction)
4 anchovy fillets in oil, drained
200g mayonnaise
1 tablespoon salted capers, drained
2 tablespoons extra virgin olive oil
2 tablespoons finely chopped flat leaf parsley leaves

These are such a great accompaniment to any main course instead of chips, or with the sauce they make a fantastic appetiser or canapé when having a party. Everyone will love them. My main tip here is to please not use tuna in brine – in my opinion that seriously is food for cats, not humans – but for this recipe in particular, it really is a no-no. Trust me, if you have no polenta chips left, you'll be using your fingers to eat the rest of the sauce.

Pour 600ml water into a saucepan with ½ teaspoon salt and bring to the boil. Slowly pour in the polenta, stirring constantly with a wooden spoon. Cook for 3–5 minutes, or according to the packet instructions. Add the butter and ½ teaspoon pepper, mix well, then add the rosemary and olive oil, mix and taste, seasoning with a little more salt and pepper to your preference.

Line a 2cm-deep baking tray with clingfilm and scrape the cooked polenta into the tray. Smooth the top and spread with a spatula or palette knife to make roughly a 25 × 8cm rectangle. Leave to cool for 10 minutes, then put in the fridge to set for 40 minutes.

Meanwhile make the sauce. Put the tuna, anchovies, mayonnaise, capers and oil in a blender. Blitz until smooth, then set aside in a small bowl.

Preheat the air fryer to 210°C for 3 minutes.

Cut the set polenta into chips each about 8 × 2cm. Place the chips in the air fryer fitted with the basket insert and cook for 20 minutes, until they are golden and crispy. Season with a generous pinch each of salt and pepper and serve with your delicious tonnata sauce on the side, sprinkled with the parsley.

DATE-NIGHT STEAKS WITH MARSALA AND SPINACH

Bistecca con rosmarino e crema di spinaci al Marsala

SERVES 2

3 tablespoons olive oil
200g large spinach leaves,
   any coarse stalks removed
2 ribeye steaks, about
   300g each, removed from
   the fridge about 1 hour
   before cooking
4 knobs of salted butter
2 rosemary sprigs
50ml Marsala wine
200ml double cream
¼ teaspoon freshly grated
   nutmeg
Salt and freshly ground
   black pepper
Sea salt flakes

Definitely a date-night dish (unless you are vegetarian!) probably because I associate the creamy Marsala sauce with my wife, as it's her favourite. Cooking steak in an air fryer is a great way to get it exactly as you like it, as the heat is consistent. A ribeye is the perfect choice too, as its fat marbling keeps the meat tender. You can substitute Marsala with Sherry or any sweet dessert wine.

Place a frying pan over a high heat and heat up the oil, then place in half the spinach. Cook for about 30 seconds, then add the remaining leaves. Sprinkle over a large pinch of salt and mix well. Cook for 2 minutes, or until it has all wilted. Tip the spinach into a sieve over a sink and press it to release excess water. Roughly chop it, then set aside.

Preheat the air fryer to 215°C for 3 minutes.

Put the steaks in the air fryer fitted with the basket insert and top each with a knob of butter and a rosemary sprig. Cook for 5 minutes. Remove the steaks from the air fryer and place on a plate.

Dab the air fryer basket insert dry with kitchen paper and let it heat up again for 1 minute. Return the steaks to the air fryer, uncooked sides down, return the rosemary sprigs, place another knob of butter on top of each and cook for a further 2–6 minutes, depending on thickness, for a rare to medium-rare steak. Add another 2 minutes for medium steaks, or 4 minutes for well-done.

Remove the steaks from the air fryer and place on a chopping board, cover with foil to keep warm and rest for 5 minutes.

Meanwhile, return the spinach to the frying pan and add the Marsala. If you're cooking on a gas hob, carefully tip the pan away from you towards the flame to ignite the alcohol, otherwise light it with a long match (be careful), so it evaporates. Cook for 30 seconds, then pour in the cream, mix together, reduce the heat to medium and let it cook for 5 minutes, stirring occasionally. Add the nutmeg, ½ teaspoon salt and ½ teaspoon pepper, stir and cook for a further 5 minutes over a low heat.

Sprinkle sea salt flakes over each rested steak. Equally divide the creamy spinach between 2 warmed plates, place the steaks on top and serve.

It is so funny how, for my family, this is by far the favourite chapter! Whenever I announce that I'm working on a new book, friends and family prepare for the wonderful (and just occasionally weird) concoctions that I might create and they always await the desserts with the most excitement. I really feel that I have a fantastic range here, catering for so many different tastes. Some of them look restaurant-standard – chocolate fondants, *millefoglie* and custard choux buns are particular showstoppers and any guest would be so impressed – yet are so easy to prepare.

My personal favourite has to be the panettone pudding and I must admit I make the apricot jam tart and the almond and raspberry tart for breakfast or tea sometimes. Served with a cup of espresso, the combination takes me to heaven.

I don't know about you guys, but most nights I don't prepare desserts as a rule. Yet working on this book reminds me that they are so easy and really do finish off a meal, so I've been asking myself why I don't make them more often. We tend only to think of making them when guests come over to eat, but who says we can't indulge every now and then? Especially when they are so simple to make in the air fryer. I am actually going to stand up and go to the kitchen now, to make one of these delicious desserts for after dinner tonight. Why? Because it's raining, because I fancy one and because we all deserve a treat!

SWEET

PAVLOVA WITH MIXED BERRIES AND DARK CHOCOLATE SAUCE

Pavlova con frutti di bosco e cioccolato fondente

SERVES 6–8

4 egg whites
200g caster sugar
1 teaspoon cornflour
300ml double cream
400g mixed berries,
    strawberries halved if large
Icing sugar, to dust

For the sauce
50g dark chocolate,
    finely chopped
10g salted butter
2½ tablespoons
    Amaretto liqueur

My wife Jessica's favourite dessert to make, as you can prepare the meringue well in advance and finish it off when people are ready to eat. It has a real wow factor, both in taste and looks: the bitter dark chocolate works perfectly with the sweet pavlova. Any berries will do, as long as they are in season, for the best flavour. You can sprinkle over some crushed pistachio nuts or hazelnuts if you fancy, too. Please don't worry if the meringue cracks a little when taking the paper off, or if it really cracks, don't panic, just call it Eton mess.

Place the egg whites in a large, very clean bowl. Whisk on a medium speed with an electric whisk until they form fluffy peaks that hold their shape. Add the sugar 1 tablespoon at a time, mixing well after each addition. Don't rush this stage, as it's what will help the meringue hold its shape. Once the sugar is all mixed through and the mixture is smooth and glossy, sprinkle the cornflour on top and mix until combined.

Preheat the air fryer to 130°C for 3 minutes. Select a 20cm diameter cake tin base from a loose-based cake tin, as you'll need the metal to cook the pavlova properly. Line the base with a circle of baking paper. Cut another long piece of baking paper to run under the tin base, to use as a 'handle' to lift the meringue in and out of the air fryer.

Set the long strip under the cake tin base, using a little meringue to stick them together. Spoon the meringue over, spreading and swirling it within the base. Gently lower into the air fryer using the long sheet of paper.

Cook for 70 minutes. Turn off the air fryer and leave the meringue inside for 1 hour. Open the drawer and wait for the meringue to cool completely before you lift it out, again using the baking paper to help you. Once it is cold, carefully peel the paper off and transfer to a serving dish.

For the sauce, place the chocolate, butter and Amaretto in a heatproof bowl and either melt in the microwave or over a small saucepan of simmering water (don't let the bowl touch the water). Mix until smooth. Set aside just for a few minutes to cool slightly, but you have to use this pretty soon, while it's still loose.

Whip the cream until it holds its shape, spoon it on the pavlova, add the berries and drizzle with the chocolate. Dust with icing sugar and serve.

HAZELNUT AND AMARETTO CANTUCCINI BISCUITS

Cantuccini

MAKES 12

125g plain flour
60g caster sugar
2 eggs
Finely grated zest of
    ½ small lemon
½ tablespoon
    Amaretto liqueur
20g unsalted butter, softened
50g whole hazelnuts

What can be more important than an espresso coffee break with a homemade biscuit to dunky-dunky? These biscuits will not disappoint, they were my Nonno Gennaro's favourite and made at least once a week at his house. They never lasted that long though. I remember once asking for a second biscuit and being told there were none left, when really Nonno was hiding them from us. I now do the same. It's important that the butter is very soft, or it will be tricky to mix. You can substitute the hazelnuts with almonds and the Amaretto with Marsala, if you prefer.

Mix the flour and sugar in a bowl.

In a separate bowl, using a whisk, beat 1 of the eggs, the lemon zest and Amaretto liqueur. Sprinkle the sugared flour on top and mix using a metal spoon: it will be a very flaky crumble-like mixture.

Add the soft butter, and, using the back of the spoon, mix well until you have made a dough. Stir the hazelnuts through. Shape the dough into a log measuring about 19 × 4cm and place on a sheet of baking paper.

Preheat the air fryer to 160°C for 3 minutes.

In a small bowl, lightly beat the remaining egg with a fork. Brush the loaf of biscuit dough with egg, place it in the air fryer fitted with the basket insert and bake for 22 minutes.

Lift out the biscuit. While still hot, carefully cut it into diagonal slices about 6mm thick (a serrated knife is good for this, as it can be a bit tricky cutting through the nuts). Lay them flat on the sheet of baking paper, return them to the air fryer and cook for a further 10–12 minutes, turning over halfway, until golden and crunchy.

Remove from the air fryer and leave them to cool completely on a wire rack. They will firm up once cooled.

PANETTONE PUDDING

Torta calda con panettone e vaniglia

SERVES 4–6

25g salted butter, melted
400ml whole milk
300ml double cream
½ vanilla pod, or 1 teaspoon
   vanilla extract
4 egg yolks
1 egg
70g caster sugar, plus
   1 tablespoon
250g panettone, cut into
   2cm slices
2 teaspoons cornflour

There are three things about this recipe which are fantastic. 1) It's my favourite dessert of all time. 2) Using panettone is amazing, as you don't have to worry about adding dried fruits and nuts as they are already in the cake. 3) Cooking it in an air fryer gives the pudding a lovely crust, yet keeps the panettone underneath from drying out. You can use a brioche loaf if you don't have panettone, but remember to add dried fruits such as raisins and candied fruits, and nuts such as almonds, in between the slices.

Grease a 20cm ovenproof dish, of about 750ml capacity, with a little of the butter.

In a saucepan, bring the milk, cream and vanilla to steaming, without letting it boil, stirring gently with a whisk, then take off the heat.

In a bowl, whisk the egg yolks, whole egg and 70g sugar with an electric whisk until smooth, then gradually whisk in the hot, creamy milk. You should have about 800ml thin custard.

Pour a thin layer of about 100ml custard into the prepared dish. The easiest way to do this is to place your baking dish on some scales and ladle in the amount needed.

Layer each panettone slice into your baking dish, building them so they overlap. Pour over 400ml more custard. Gently push the panettone down, allowing the slices to absorb the custard. Leave to soak for 10 minutes, then gently push the slices down again.

Preheat the air fryer to 160C for 3 minutes.

Cook for 15 minutes. Brush the remaining butter on top, sprinkle over the 1 tablespoon sugar and cook for a further 5 minutes until golden. Remove and allow to rest for 5 minutes.

Meanwhile, pour the remaining custard back into the saucepan and set over a medium heat. Mix the cornflour with 2 tablespoons water in a small cup until smooth, then add to the custard. Using a whisk, stir for 4 minutes until it thickens. Remove from the heat and generously pour it over a huge helping of panettone pudding. If you aren't ready to serve, press clingfilm on the custard's surface, so it doesn't form a skin.

RHUBARB CRUMBLE WITH LIMONCELLO

Sbriciolata con rabarbaro e limoncello

SERVES 2

75g plain flour
75g granulated sugar
50g cold salted butter, cut into
   cubes, plus more for the dish
380g rhubarb, cut into
   3cm lengths
2 tablespoons limoncello

This is my father-in-law Malcolm's favourite dessert, so I am going to dedicate this recipe to him. I know it isn't very Italian, but to me this is just what a simple dessert should look and taste like. It is very very easy to make and a fantastic recipe for beginners. You can substitute the rhubarb with apples and the limoncello with Cointreau if you prefer. Make sure you leave some big pieces in the mixture when making the crumble, as they will give a lovely extra crunch. I like to serve this with homemade custard (see previous page) or double cream instead of ice cream sometimes. Any one of them – or even all three – work amazingly.

Mix the flour and 30g of the sugar in a bowl, add the cold butter cubes and rub together with your fingertips until it looks like very coarse crumbs; some chunky bits are good.

Preheat the air fryer to 170°C for 3 minutes.

Lightly grease a baking dish about 20cm in diameter that fits the air fryer.

Place the rhubarb in the dish, sprinkle the remaining sugar all over, then top with the crumble, spreading it out evenly even if some lands on the rim. Drizzle the limoncello over, then cook the crumble for 22 minutes, or until golden and bubbling.

Serve immediately with scoops of creamy vanilla ice cream.

FERRERO ROCHER CUPCAKES

Tortini di Ferrero Rocher

MAKES 6

For the cupcakes
100g salted butter, softened
30g cocoa powder
40ml hot water
1 egg
100g caster sugar
100g self-raising flour

For the topping
90g chocolate-hazelnut
   spread, such as Nutella,
   at room temperature
6 Ferrero Rocher
50g chopped hazelnuts
150g milk chocolate, finely
   chopped
Edible gold glitter spray
   (optional)

As many people know, Ferrero Rocher are my favourite chocolates of all time, so I had to come up with a recipe to incorporate them somehow, and here it is. I've tried this recipe with other chocolates, such as Baci Perugina, and it works equally well. If you fancy making the cakes a little boozy, you can add 2 tablespoons Amaretto liqueur to the cupcake mixture, and you can substitute the chopped hazelnuts with almonds or walnuts if you prefer.

Melt the butter in a small bowl in the microwave, add the cocoa and measured hot water and mix well to make a paste. Allow to cool for 5 minutes.

With an electric whisk, beat the egg and sugar in a bowl for 5 minutes until light and creamy. Fold in the flour with a wooden spoon, followed by the cocoa mixture. Divide between 6 cupcake cases; I used gold paper cases set inside silicone cupcake cases while they were baking.

Preheat the air fryer to 140°C for 3 minutes.

Cook for 12 minutes until the cupcakes spring back to the touch of a finger. Set aside to cool.

Blob 1 teaspoon chocolate-hazelnut spread in the centre of each cooled cupcake. Using a palette knife, gently spread more of it all over the Ferrero Rocher, then set one on top of each cupcake, on the blob of spread. Sprinkle the hazelnuts on top, using your hands to lightly press them in, so they stick.

Melt the chocolate in a small bowl in the microwave, let it cool for 5 minutes, then spoon the melted chocolate over each cupcake, starting in the middle of the Ferrero Rocher, then spooning around the edges of each, so the melted chocolate drips down to roughly cover the Rocher.

Leave somewhere cool to set for about 30 minutes, Get creative if you like and dust with gold glitter, then make a cup of tea and enjoy.

APRICOT JAM TART WITH LEMON ZEST

Crostata di marmellata alle albicocche e scorzetta di limone

SERVES 6

70g unsalted butter, softened, plus more for the pie plate or tart tin
40g caster sugar
Finely grated zest of ½ small lemon
Salt
160g plain flour, plus more to dust
½ teaspoon baking powder
1 egg, lightly beaten
225g apricot jam
Icing sugar, to dust

This was my father Ciro's favourite tart of all time. It is such an Italian classic that you can buy it almost everywhere in Italy and yet it is so satisfying to create yourself. If you have children, get them involved; they love rolling out the pastry and cutting and placing on the strips in a lattice. I have used apricot jam as it's the traditional choice and goes really well with the buttery pastry, but strawberry jam also works fantastically. This can be eaten warm, at room temperature, or even (my favourite) cold for breakfast.

Grease a 20cm pie plate or tart tin.

In a bowl, beat the softened butter and sugar until smooth, using an electric whisk, for about 2 minutes. Put in the lemon zest and a pinch of salt and continue to beat for another minute.

Mix the flour and baking powder in a separate bowl, then add them to the butter mixture and mix together using the back of a metal spoon until it looks like sand. Add the egg and whisk until combined, about 2 minutes. It will still be lumpy and that's the way it should be, so don't be tempted to overmix it. Bring together into a ball with your hands, then tip on to a work surface dusted with flour and gently work into a dough.

Roll two-thirds of the pastry out to a circle 3mm thick (set the rest aside). Loosely roll the pastry around the rolling pin, then carefully unroll it over the prepared plate or tin. Press gently into the corners and loosely around all sides. Trim the pastry to give you a neat 1.5cm overhang all around.

Roll the rest of the pastry into a 25 × 12cm rectangle, again about 3mm thick, and cut it into 2cm strips.

Fill the tart tin with the apricot jam and set the pastry strips on top in a criss-cross pattern. Gently turn the pastry overhang from the base over the top edges of the lattice, creating a crust.

Preheat the air fryer to 200°C for 3 minutes to get it really hot.

Reduce the air fryer temperature to 160°C and then cook the tart for 40 minutes, until the jam is bubbling and the pastry is cooked through. Remove and let it stand for 20 minutes before dusting with icing sugar and slicing.

RICOTTA AND PANETTONE CHEESECAKE WITH CHOCOLATE CHIPS

Torta con ricotta, panettone e cioccolato

SERVES 4–6

Butter, for the tin
2 eggs
2 egg yolks
75g caster sugar
⅛ teaspoon fine sea salt
60g crème fraîche
25g plain flour
350g ricotta
1 teaspoon vanilla extract
  (or see recipe introduction)
50g chocolate chips
70g panettone chunks or slices
Icing sugar, to serve

This isn't a traditional cheesecake as we know it; for a start, it doesn't have a biscuit base, and it has more of a cake-like centre, too. Using ricotta gives this dessert a lovely lightness, perfect with the sweetness of panettone. I came up with the recipe in January, after having lots of bits of leftover panettone from Christmas. I simply put the leftover chunks into a cheesecake mixture… and here we are. I just love creating new recipes from leftovers and coming up with magic. You can substitute the vanilla extract with Amaretto liqueur, if you prefer.

Line an 18cm cake tin with baking paper, then grease it with the butter.

In a bowl, beat the eggs and egg yolks with the sugar and salt using an electric whisk. Beat for about 4 minutes, until thick and fluffy.

In a small bowl, using a whisk, mix the crème fraîche with the flour until smooth, then mix in the ricotta and vanilla extract, again until smooth. Scrape this into the egg mixture and gently whisk together on the lowest speed until combined.

Preheat the air fryer to 150°C for 3 minutes.

Sprinkle half the chocolate chips into the prepared tin and pour in the egg mixture. Place the panettone chunks or slices on top and dot the remaining chocolate chips over. Cover the top tightly with foil, sealing it around the rim, then bake for 30 minutes. Remove the foil and bake for a further 15 minutes.

Once cooked, allow to rest: the cheesecake will have a slight wobble in the middle when it comes out of the air fryer, but it will firm up as it cools. Once cooled, place in the fridge for at least 1 hour. To serve, take out of the fridge 20 minutes before serving and dust with icing sugar.

MILLEFEUILLE WITH STRAWBERRIES, AMARETTO AND PISTACHIOS

Millefoglie con fragole, Amaretto e pistacchi

SERVES 5

320g sheet of puff pastry,
    frozen flat on a tray for
    20 minutes (this means you
    can cut out sharper pieces)
1 egg, lightly beaten
1 tablespoon icing sugar
400g strawberries
3 tablespoons Amaretto liqueur

For the filling
150g mascarpone
300ml double cream
2 tablespoons icing sugar,
    plus more to dust
1 teaspoon vanilla extract
40g chopped pistachio nuts

Fantastic to serve at a summer party or barbecue with a cheeky glass of cold prosecco. When strawberries are in season, they are so super-sweet and tasty, but, if they aren't in season, use any seasonal berries you like. If you prefer, you can substitute the Amaretto liqueur with rum or limoncello. You can also change the pistachio nuts for hazelnuts or walnuts, it's up to you, all work great.

Cut the pastry into 10 rectangles, each about 11 × 6cm. Prick them all over with a fork and keep in the fridge on a tray lined with baking paper.

Preheat the air fryer to 190°C for 3 minutes.

Cut out 2 sheets of baking paper, each the width of the air fryer drawer but slightly longer, so you can lift the pastry out using the extra paper as 'handles'. You'll need to cook these in 3–4 batches. Put 1 sheet of baking paper into the air fryer drawer and place about 3 pastry pieces on top, with space between them. Cover with the other sheet of baking paper. Gently place a 20cm cake tin (or the air fryer basket insert, if it's flat) on top, to weigh the pastry down, so it rises evenly. Cook for 8 minutes.

Remove the cake tin or basket insert and the upper sheet of baking paper, brush with a little egg, dust with a little of the icing sugar, then bake for a further 6 minutes until golden and cooked through. As each batch is done, carefully lift it out using the paper, transfer to a wire rack to cool and reuse the paper and method for the remaining pastries.

Meanwhile, trim the tops off the strawberries and slice about two-thirds of the largest berries into 5mm slices. Halve the rest. Place all the berries in a bowl with the Amaretto, stir gently and set aside.

For the filling, place the mascarpone in a bowl and loosen the consistency by beating lightly with a rubber spatula. Pour in the cream, icing sugar and vanilla extract and whip with a whisk until smooth.

Very gently (you don't want to break the delicate pastry), spread or pipe a layer of the filling on all the pastry rectangles with a palette knife, then sprinkle over the sliced strawberries and pistachios. Place half the most attractive pastries on top of the messier half, creating 5 double-layered millefoglie. Dust with icing sugar and serve immediately.

ALMOND AND RASPBERRY FRANGIPANE TART

Crostata frangipane alle mandorle e lamponi

SERVES 4

2 eggs
320g sheet of puff pastry
  (you'll use half)
50g salted butter, at room
  temperature
50g caster sugar
75g ground almonds
50g raspberries
15g flaked almonds
Icing sugar, to dust

My secret midnight feast will often feature an almond slice, so I created something super-quick and similar in taste, as I just love the flavours. I must stress that it's important to cook the pastry in the air fryer fitted with the basket insert, so the air circulates around it, making the pastry lovely and crispy underneath. Using a piping bag isn't essential, you could spread the frangipane with a palette knife, or dot it on and spread with a wet spoon (wet so the frangipane doesn't stick).

Preheat the air fryer to 180°C for 3 minutes.

Lightly beat 1 egg in a small bowl and set aside.

Unroll the puff pastry sheet with a long side closest to you. Trim a 3cm strip from the end (so it fits in your air fryer). Cut the remaining sheet in half to get two 19cm squares. Wrap and freeze one of the squares and the trimmings for another time. (You can use them to make my Asparagus, Gorgonzola and honey tart, see page 157.)

Run a knife around the edge of the pastry to lightly score a 2cm border, then prick the pastry all over the middle section with a fork. Brush with some of the beaten egg, carefully set in the air fryer fitted with the basket insert and cook for 25 minutes.

Meanwhile, make the frangipane. Place the butter, sugar, remaining egg and 1 tablespoon of the ground almonds in a small mixing bowl and beat with an electric whisk for 2–3 minutes until light and fluffy. Add the remaining ground almonds and beat for a further minute until smooth. Transfer to a piping bag (or see recipe introduction).

Lift out the pastry from the air fryer and set on a work surface. Reduce the air fryer temperature to 160°C.

Pipe or spread the frangipane within the border of the pastry, place the raspberries on top, then the flaked almonds. Cook for 16 minutes.

Carefully lift out your tart, place on a plate and dust with icing sugar. Serve a slice with whipped cream or ice cream, if you fancy.

ITALIAN CUSTARD CHOUX BUN WITH AMARENA CHERRIES

Zeppole di San Giuseppe

MAKES 6

For the filling
75g caster sugar
4 egg yolks
20g cornflour
1½ teaspoons vanilla extract
325ml whole milk
80ml double cream

For the pastry
125ml water
50g unsalted butter, cut
   into cubes
Salt
75g plain flour
2 eggs

To serve
Amarena cherries in syrup
Icing sugar

Every time my sister Marcella visits me in the UK, I always make these for her, as they are her ultimate favourite. I know that it looks like a fairly long process, but don't be put off by the steps, it's not difficult and the results are insane. *Zeppole di San Giuseppe* are made to celebrate the feast of Saint Joseph and Father's Day, and the patisseries in Italy are filled with these delights during that time. You can substitute the Amarena cherries for any kind of cherries in syrup and, of course, once you have mastered the choux buns, chocolate or toffee sauce are both a must-try with them.

To make the filling, whisk the sugar, egg yolks, cornflour and vanilla extract in a bowl until smooth. Set aside.

Heat the milk in a saucepan over a medium heat until very hot but not boiling. Pour the hot milk slowly over the flour mixture, stirring constantly with a whisk. Pour the custard back into the saucepan, set over a medium heat and keep whisking. It will become slightly lumpy, but just keep whisking until the custard is smooth, thick and glossy, and the cornflour is absorbed, about 3 minutes.

Remove from the heat and transfer to a medium bowl or jug. Cover the surface of the custard with clingfilm so it doesn't form a skin. Allow to cool, then put in the fridge to chill until needed.

Meanwhile, cut a piece of baking paper to fit inside the air fryer drawer. Draw six 5cm circles evenly spaced out on it, to use as a guide when piping the pastry out. Set aside.

For the pastry, put the measured water into a saucepan with the butter and a pinch of salt. Place over a medium heat until the butter melts, then bring to the boil. Reduce the heat to medium and add the flour all at once. Stir until the flour is completely incorporated, then beat with a wooden spoon for 2 minutes. Take off the heat and continue to mix all the time until it transforms into a smooth, thick paste. Let it cool for 3 minutes, then beat in the eggs one at a time.

Preheat the air fryer to 180°C for 3 minutes.

Using a piping bag, pipe the *zeppole* into the drawn circles on the paper, directly into the air fryer drawer. As a guide, each should be about 3.5cm tall and within the stencilled circle, so you need to pipe a blob rather than a swirl, keeping the piping bag in the same spot and moving it up gradually as you pipe.

Cook for 12 minutes.

Increase the air fryer temperature to 200°C and cook the *zeppole* for a further 14 minutes. Remove and allow to cool.

Once the buns and filling have cooled and you are ready to assemble, add the cream to the custard and beat with an electric whisk until smooth and thick. Spoon the filling into a piping bag fitted with a star nozzle.

Slice the tops off the choux to create deeper bases and shallower lids. Generously fill each pastry base with the filling. Put the pastry lids back on top, then pipe a peak of the custard on the lids, too. Place a cherry on top and dust with icing sugar if you want a bit of extra sweetness.

Pop one in your mouth and enjoy!

LEMON AND ALMOND POLENTA CAKE

Torta di polenta, limoni e mandorle

SERVES 6

125g unsalted butter, softened and cubed, plus more for the tin
100g ground almonds
115g fine polenta
Fine salt
1 level teaspoon baking powder
175g caster sugar
2 eggs
Finely grated zest and juice of 2 small lemons (or see recipe introduction)
75ml whole milk

This is really special to me, not only because it was one of my mother's specialities, but also because it was a traditional cake made every Easter Sunday without fail. I remember waking up to the aroma of it baking, and, to this day, it takes me back in time. Dessert, afternoon tea or – even better – a breakfast slice: perfect perfect *perfect*! Make sure to buy fine polenta or cornmeal rather than regular, and your butter must be soft so it combines easily. You can substitute the lemon juice with limoncello liqueur, if you prefer.

Grease a 16 × 9 × 7cm loaf tin and line it with baking paper.

Put the almonds, polenta, a pinch of salt, the baking powder and 115g of the sugar in a bowl and stir, so the dry ingredients are evenly mixed.

Make a well in the middle, crack in the eggs, add the butter, lemon zest and milk and beat on a medium speed with an electric whisk for about 3 minutes, working all the dry ingredients in from the sides to create a smooth batter.

Preheat the air fryer to 160°C for 3 minutes.

Pour the mixture into the prepared tin, flatten the top and bake for 20 minutes.

Reduce the air fryer temperature to 150°C and cook for a further 25 minutes, or for a couple of minutes less if your tin is slightly bigger and the batter is less deep, until cooked through and golden. You can check this by putting a cocktail stick or skewer in the middle of your cake, to make sure it comes out clean.

Meanwhile, mix the lemon juice and remaining 60g sugar in a jug, to dissolve. When the cake has cooled for 5 minutes, gradually brush or spoon the sugar mixture evenly all over until absorbed. Cool for 10 minutes in the tin, then turn out to cool completely on a wire rack.

PERFECT AIR FRYER CHOCOLATE FONDANTS

Tortini caldi ripieni di cioccolato

SERVES 4

100g butter, cubed, plus more
    for the moulds
Cocoa powder, to dust
125g dark chocolate, finely
    chopped
180g caster sugar
½ teaspoon fine sea salt
3 eggs
90g plain flour
Vanilla ice cream, double
    cream or mascarpone,
    to serve

This recipe for little chocolate delights is dedicated to my son Rocco, as it's his favourite dessert of all time. For all you chocolate lovers out there, it is a must-try. These are fantastic if you are entertaining guests and want to impress, as you can get them ready and cook when needed. They will happily sit at room temperature for two hours, waiting for a hot dessert to order... You're welcome!

Grease 4 × 175ml mini pudding moulds with butter and dust with cocoa powder, tipping away any excess.

Place a saucepan of water over a medium heat and bring to a simmer. Place a heatproof bowl on top, ensuring it doesn't touch the water, then gently melt the chocolate and cubed butter together until smooth (you can also melt them in a microwave if you prefer). Use a plastic spatula to stir and combine.

Take off the heat, stir in the sugar and salt and allow to cool slightly. Whisk in the eggs one by one with an electric whisk on a medium-low speed. Mix in the flour on a low speed until smooth.

Equally pour the chocolate mix into the prepared moulds. They can stand at room temperature for 2 hours at this stage.

Preheat the air fryer to 170°C for 3 minutes.

Place the fondants in the air fryer and bake for 11 minutes. Remove and leave to stand for 2 minutes.

Carefully run a knife around the edges to loosen, then turn out on to dessert plates. Serve with a generous dollop of vanilla ice cream, double cream – or my personal favourite – mascarpone.

ACKNOWLEDGEMENTS

I would like to start by thanking my managers, Luciano and Rocco D'Acampo and the team at MeMs Agency. What an incredible journey it has been so far – it is an absolute privilege and honour to be represented by you. As your father, proud is not a big enough word for what I feel. Thank you!

Huge love to the girls in my life: my wife Jessica, who tested all the recipes, and my beautiful daughter Mia, who eats them all. Coming home to your cuddles, after a long day's work, makes it all worthwhile.

A big thank you to everybody at Bloomsbury Publishing. This is our third book together and, once again, it's been a pleasure working with you all. A special mention to Lena Hall, Rowan Yapp, Rose Brown, Laura Brodie in Production, Diana Riley in Marketing, Sarah Bennie in PR and to Lucy Bannell, my editor. I'd also like to give massive thanks to Katy McClelland, my fantastic home economist on this book, for all your hard work and commitment on this new adventure of air fryers. Thanks to Liz and Max at Haarala Hamilton for the beautiful photos, Jennifer Kay for the lovely props and Anna Green for the amazing design.

I couldn't write an acknowledgement page without mentioning the super-cool people at Asda. Together we have created an incredible air fryer range that makes all my Italian creations come true in one or two little drawers, who knew?! May we continue to create new wonderful things together.

A massive thank you goes to my home country, Italy, which, over the years, has taught me new recipes and keeps inspiring me with new flavours and new dishes. I love the people I meet while filming my TV shows, the markets I shop in, the regions I visit and the food I taste. All of it is a huge contribution to my success and I'll be forever grateful to my *Italia*.

The biggest thank you goes to my fans. I am honestly forever grateful to all of you, who over the past 20 years have continued to ride this journey with me. May we continue to laugh together, drink together and eat together for many years to come. A big kiss to all of you.

Grazie xxx

CONVERSION TABLES

WEIGHTS

METRIC	IMPERIAL
15g	½oz
20g	¾oz
30g	1oz
55g	2oz
85g	3oz
110g	4oz / ¼lb
140g	5oz
170g	6oz
200g	7oz
225g	8oz / ½lb
255g	9oz
285g	10oz
310g	11oz
340g	12oz / ¾lb
370g	13oz
400g	14oz
425g	15oz
450g	16oz / 1lb
1kg	2lb 4oz
1.5kg	3lb 5oz

USEFUL CONVERSIONS

1 tablespoon = 3 teaspoons
1 (UK medium) egg = 53–63g / 2oz
UK large egg = US extra-large egg

LIQUIDS

METRIC	IMPERIAL
5ml	1 teaspoon
15ml	1 tablespoon or ½fl oz
30ml	2 tablespoons or 1fl oz
150ml	¼ pint or 5fl oz
290ml	½ pint or 10fl oz
425ml	¾ pint or 16fl oz
570ml	1 pint or 20fl oz
1 litre	1 ¾ pints
1.2 litres	2 pints

LENGTH

METRIC	IMPERIAL
5mm	¼ in
1cm	½in
2cm	¾in
2.5cm	1in
5cm	2in
10cm	4in
15cm	6in
20cm	8in
30cm	12in

OVEN TEMPERATURES

°C	°C FAN	GAS MARK	°F
110°C	90°C fan	Gas mark ¼	225°F
120°C	100°C fan	Gas mark ½	250°F
140°C	120°C fan	Gas mark 1	275°F
150°C	130°C fan	Gas mark 2	300°F
160°C	140°C fan	Gas mark 3	325°F
180°C	160°C fan	Gas mark 4	350°F
190°C	170°C fan	Gas mark 5	375°F
200°C	180°C fan	Gas mark 6	400°F
220°C	200°C fan	Gas mark 7	425°F
230°C	210°C fan	Gas mark 8	450°F
240°C	220°C fan	Gas mark 9	475°F

INDEX

A

ali di pollo alla diavola caramellizzate al miele 87

almonds: almond and raspberry frangipane tart 189

lemon and almond polenta cake 194

Amaretto: hazelnut and Amaretto cantuccini biscuits 174

millefeuille with strawberries, Amaretto and pistachios 186

anchovies: roast leg of lamb with rosemary, fennel and pepper 122

salsa tonnata 165

apricot jam: apricot and rosemary glazed chicken 102

apricot jam tart with lemon zest 183

arancine: crispy arancine with ham and mozzarella 34

arancine con prosciutto cotto e mozzarella 34

arrosto di maiale con latte e salvia 50

asparagus, Gorgonzola and honey tart 157

aubergines: aubergine Parmigiana with spiced tomato and oozing mozzarella 40

Aunty Clara's stuffed aubergines with lentils and mozzarella 141

bucatini with aubergine, tomatoes and toasted almonds 134

crispy cheesy aubergine bites 94

Sicilian aubergines with red wine vinegar and green olives 18

Aunty Clara's stuffed aubergines with lentils and mozzarella 141

B

beef: Bolognese-style sauce 23

classic lasagne 24

date-night steaks with Marsala and spinach 166

Italian meatloaf with Parma ham and Provolone cheese 46

roasted stuffed peppers with Bolognese sauce and mozzarella 79

succulent meatballs with spicy tomato sauce 31

topside tagliata with rocket, Parmesan and balsamic 39

berries: pavlova with mixed berries and dark chocolate sauce 170

bistecca con rosmarino e crema di spinaci al Marsala 166

bocconcini croccanti di melanzane e formaggio 94

Bolognese-style sauce 23

classic lasagne 24

roasted stuffed peppers with 79

brandied turkey breast 112

bread: bruschetta with marinated tomatoes and creamy burrata 150

garlic bread 57

panzanella salad with king prawns and ciabatta 63

toasted 'raid the deli' picnic panino 69

brioche: succulent chicken burgers 90

bruschetta con pomodori marinate e burrata 150

bruschetta with marinated tomatoes and creamy burrata 150

bucatini con salsa di melanzane, pomodori freschi e mandorle tostate 134

bucatini with aubergine, tomatoes and toasted almonds 134

burgers, succulent chicken 90

burgers di pollo con rucola e parmigiano 90

C

cabbage: slaw 144

cakes: Ferrero Rocher cupcakes 180

lemon and almond polenta cake 194

cannelloni ricotta e spinaci 16

cannelloni with spinach and ricotta 16

cantuccini 174

cantuccini biscuits, hazelnut and Amaretto 174

caponata alla Siciliana 18

carbonara potatoes 100

cauliflower: whole roast cauliflower with Calabrian chillies and lemon zest 106

cavolfiore intero arrostito con pepperoncini Calabrese e scorzetta di limone 106

ceci croccanti con aglio e finocchietto 80

cheese: asparagus, Gorgonzola and honey tart 157

aubergine Parmigiana with spiced tomato and oozing mozzarella 40

Aunty Clara's stuffed aubergines with lentils and mozzarella 141

baked pasta with sausages, garlic, rosemary and mozzarella 84

bruschetta with marinated tomatoes and creamy burrata 150

carbonara potatoes 100

chicken involtini with ham and smoked mozzarella 76

chicken Kyiv with sage and pecorino Romano 152

courgette and fontina tart 20

crispy arancine with ham and mozzarella 34

crispy cheesy aubergine bites 94

four cheese maccheroni 88

gnocchi in pancetta, tomato and Parmesan sauce 108

gnocchi with tomato, mozzarella and basil 28

golden croquettes with mozzarella and ham 116

Italian meatloaf with Parma ham and Provolone cheese 46

lasagne with pistachios, Parma ham and mozzarella 161

Mortadella, sour cherry, fontina and red onion sausage rolls 99

pizza chicken breasts 66

pizza puff sticks 72

potato cake 36

roasted pumpkin lasagne 119

roasted stuffed peppers with Bolognese sauce and mozzarella 79

Roman-style gnocchi with pecorino Romano 44

Roman-style pizza with olives and semi-dried tomatoes 105

smashed potatoes with speck ham and Gorgonzola 110

spaghetti frittata with courgettes and pecorino Romano 133

succulent chicken burgers with rocket and Parmesan 90

toasted 'raid the deli' picnic panino 69

topside tagliata 39

see also mascarpone; ricotta cheese

cheesecake, ricotta and panettone 184

cherries: Italian custard choux bun with Amarena cherries 190–1

Mortadella, sour cherry, fontina and red onion sausage rolls 99

chicken: apricot and rosemary glazed chicken 102

chicken involtini with ham and smoked mozzarella 76

chicken Kyiv with sage and pecorino Romano 152

chicken legs with potatoes, lemons and capers 136

chicken saltimbocca with Parma ham, sage and Marsala 52

chicken with saffron-lemon sauce 158

devilled chicken wings with smoked paprika and honey 87

pizza chicken breasts 66
polenta-crusted chicken breasts with
chilli and lemon zest 142
succulent chicken burgers with rocket
and Parmesan 90
chickpeas, crispy 80
chillies: devilled chicken wings 87
giardiniera relish 69
polenta-crusted chicken breasts with
chilli and lemon zest 142
spicy glazed pork chops with hot honey
and slaw 144
whole roast cauliflower with Calabrian
chillies and lemon zest 106
chips, super-crispy polenta 165
chocolate: Ferrero Rocher cupcakes 180
pavlova with mixed berries and dark
chocolate sauce 170
perfect air fryer chocolate fondants 196
ricotta and panettone cheesecake with
chocolate chips 184
choux buns: Italian custard choux bun with
Amarena cherries 190–1
cod: creamy fish pie with parsley, garlic
and lemon gremolata 96
honey-glazed cod with lemon and
garlic 60
*cosce di pollo con patate al limone e
capperi* 136
*coscia di agnello arrosto con rosmarino,
finocchietto e pepe nero* 122
*costine di maiale con patate e rosmarino di
nonna Assunta* 115
*costolette di agnello con pancetta, piselli e
miele* 162
*costolette di maiale glassate con 'nduja e
miele* 144
courgettes: baked ricotta and courgettes
with rosemary and pistachio nuts 58
courgette and fontina tart 20
courgette fries 64
sliced courgettes with mint, garlic and
white wine vinegar 26
spaghetti frittata with courgettes and
pecorino Romano 133
cream: carbonara potatoes 100
panettone pudding 177
pavlova with mixed berries and dark
chocolate sauce 170
creamy fish pie 96
crispy arancine with ham and mozzarella 34
crispy cheesy aubergine bites 94
crispy chickpeas with garlic and fennel
seeds 80
crispy-crackling pork loin in milk and sage 50
crispy rosemary-crusted pork loin chops 75
*crocchette di patate con mozzarella filante
e prosciutto cotto* 116
croquettes: golden croquettes with
mozzarella and ham 116

*crostata di marmellata alle albicocche e
scorzetta di limone* 183
*crostata frangipane alle mandorle e
lamponi* 189
crumble, rhubarb 178
custard: Italian custard choux bun with
Amarena cherries 190–1

D

date-night steaks with Marsala and spinach
166
devilled chicken wings 87

E

eggs: my healthy hangover brunch
120
Scotch egg with Martini Bianco 93
spaghetti frittata with courgettes and
pecorino Romano 133

F

fennel salad 148
Ferrero Rocher cupcakes 180
fish: creamy fish pie with parsley, garlic and
lemon gremolata 96
honey-glazed cod with lemon and
garlic 60
Mediterranean-style salmon with olives
and cherry tomatoes 130
salsa tonnata 165
whole sea bream with lemon and
prosecco 148
fondants, perfect air fryer chocolate
196
frangipane: almond and raspberry
frangipane tart 189
fries, courgette 64
frittata: spaghetti frittata with courgettes and
pecorino Romano 133
*frittata di spaghetti con zucchine e pecorino
Romano* 133

G

garlic bread with parsley and smoked
paprika 57
gâteau di patate 36
giardiniera relish 69
gnocchi: gnocchi in pancetta, tomato and
Parmesan sauce 108
Roman-style gnocchi with pecorino
Romano 44
gnocchi alla Romana 44
gnocchi alla Sorrentina 28
gnocchi with tomato, mozzarella and basil
28
golden croquettes with mozzarella and
ham 116
gremolata 96, 158
grissini di sfoglia alla pizzaiola 72
guanciale: carbonara potatoes 100

H

ham: chicken involtini with ham and smoked
mozzarella 76
crispy arancine with ham and
mozzarella 34
golden croquettes with mozzarella and
ham 116
potato cake 36
see also Parma ham; speck
hazelnuts: Ferrero Rocher cupcakes 180
hazelnut and Amaretto cantuccini biscuits 174

I

*insalatona panzanella con gamberoni e
ciabatta* 63
involtini: chicken involtini with ham and
smoked mozzarella 76
involtini di pollo con prosciutto e formaggio
76
Italian custard choux bun with Amarena
cherries 190–1
Italian meatloaf with Parma ham and
Provolone cheese 46

K

kebabs, lamb 138
Kyiv: chicken Kyiv with sage and pecorino
Romano 152

L

lamb: lamb chops with crispy pancetta,
peas and honey 162
lamb kebabs 138
roast leg of lamb with rosemary, fennel
and pepper 122
Scotch egg with Martini Bianco 93
lasagne: classic lasagne 24
lasagne with pistachios, Parma ham and
mozzarella 161
roasted pumpkin lasagne 119
lasagne alla Bolognese 24
*lasagne con pistacchi, prosciutto crudo e
mozzarella* 161
*lasagne di zucca arrostita con besciamella
cremosa* 119
lemons: apricot jam tart with lemon zest 183
chicken legs with potatoes, lemons and
capers 136
chicken supremes with saffron-lemon
sauce 158
creamy fish pie with parsley, garlic and
lemon gremolata 96
honey-glazed cod with lemon and
garlic 60
lemon and almond polenta cake 194
polenta-crusted chicken breasts with
chilli and lemon zest 142
whole roast cauliflower with Calabrian
chillies and lemon zest 106

whole sea bream with lemon and prosecco, with fennel salad 148
lentils: Aunty Clara's stuffed aubergines with lentils and mozzarella 141
limoncello, rhubarb crumble with 178
lombo di maiale alla Milanese 75

M

maccheroni, four cheese 88
maccheroni ai quattro formaggi 88
Marsala: chicken saltimbocca with Parma ham, sage and Marsala 52
date-night steaks with Marsala and spinach 166
Martini Bianco, Scotch egg with 93
mascarpone: four cheese maccheroni 88
millefeuille with strawberries, Amaretto and pistachios 186
mayonnaise: salsa tonnata 165
meatballs: succulent meatballs with spicy tomato sauce 31
meatloaf: Italian meatloaf with Parma ham and Provolone cheese 46
Mediterranean-style salmon with olives and cherry tomatoes 130
melanzane alla Parmigiana 40
melanzane ripiene di zia Clara con lenticchie e mozzarella 141
meringues: pavlova with mixed berries and dark chocolate sauce 170
merluzzo alla Sorrentina con aglio, miele e limone 60
Milanese-style air fryer risotto with saffron and wine 33
milk: crispy-crackling pork loin in milk and sage 50
millefeuille with strawberries, Amaretto and pistachios 186
millefoglie con fragole, Amaretto e pistacchi 186
Mortadella: Mortadella, sour cherry, fontina and red onion sausage rolls 99
toasted 'raid the deli' picnic panino 69
my healthy hangover brunch 120
my Nonna Assunta's pork ribs with potatoes and rosemary 115

O

oils, choosing 10
olives: giardiniera relish 69
Mediterranean-style salmon with olives and cherry tomatoes 130
Roman-style pizza with olives and semi-dried tomatoes 105
Sicilian aubergines with red wine vinegar and green olives 18
onions: Mortadella, sour cherry, fontina and red onion sausage rolls 99
orate intera con limone, prosecco e finocchio 148

P

pancetta: Bolognese-style sauce 23
gnocchi in pancetta, tomato and Parmesan sauce 108
lamb chops with crispy pancetta, peas and honey 162
my healthy hangover brunch 120
pane all'aglio, prezzemolo e paprika 57
panettone: panettone pudding 177
ricotta and panettone cheesecake with chocolate chips 184
panino, toasted 'raid the deli' picnic 69
panino tostato ripieno con giardiniera e affettati 69
panzanella salad with king prawns and ciabatta 63
Parma ham: chicken saltimbocca with Parma ham, sage and Marsala 52
Italian meatloaf with Parma ham and Provolone cheese 46
lasagne with pistachios, Parma ham and mozzarella 161
toasted 'raid the deli' picnic panino 69
Parmigiana, aubergine 40
pasta: baked pasta with sausages, garlic, rosemary and mozzarella 84
Bolognese-style sauce 23
bucatini with aubergine, tomatoes and toasted almonds 134
cannelloni with spinach and ricotta 16
classic lasagne 24
four cheese maccheroni with extra-crispy topping 88
lasagne with pistachios, Parma ham and mozzarella 161
roasted pumpkin lasagne 119
spaghetti frittata with courgettes and pecorino Romano 133
pasta al forno 84
patate al forno stile carbonara con guanciale e parmigiano 100
patate arrosto con uova, timo e pancetta 120
patate schiacciate con speck e gorgonzola 110
pavlova con frutti di bosco e cioccolato fondente 170
pavlova with mixed berries and dark chocolate sauce 170
peas: lamb chops with crispy pancetta, peas and honey 162
peperoni arrostiti 49
peperoni ripieni con sugo alla Bolognese e mozzarella 79
peppers: lamb kebabs 138
roasted peppers with parsley, garlic and extra virgin olive oil 49
roasted stuffed peppers with Bolognese sauce and mozzarella 79

petti di pollo in crosta di polenta al pepperoncino e limone 142
petto di pollo ripieno di burro alla salvia, aglio e pecorino Romano 152
petto di tacchino al burro e brandy 112
pie, creamy fish 96
pistachios: baked ricotta and courgettes with rosemary and pistachio nuts 58
lasagne with pistachios, Parma ham and mozzarella 161
millefeuille with strawberries, Amaretto and pistachios 186
pizza: pizza chicken breasts 66
pizza puff sticks 72
Roman-style pizza with olives and semi-dried tomatoes 105
pizza alla Romana con mozzarella, olive e pomodori semi-secchi 105
polenta: lemon and almond polenta cake 194
polenta-crusted chicken breasts 142
super-crispy polenta chips with salsa tonnata 165
pollo alla pizzaiola con mozzarella filante 66
pollo arrosto con rosmarino e marmellata di albicocche 102
polpette di carne al Martini Bianco ripiene d'uovo 93
polpettone classico con prosciutto crudo e formaggio 46
pork: Bolognese-style sauce 23
classic lasagne 24
crispy-crackling pork loin in milk and sage 50
crispy rosemary-crusted pork loin chops 75
Italian meatloaf with Parma ham and Provolone cheese 46
my Nonna Assunta's pork ribs with potatoes and rosemary 115
roasted stuffed peppers with Bolognese sauce and mozzarella 79
Scotch egg with Martini Bianco 93
spicy glazed pork chops with hot honey and slaw 144
succulent meatballs with spicy tomato sauce 31
see also sausages
potato gnocchi: gnocchi in pancetta, tomato and Parmesan sauce 108
gnocchi with tomato, mozzarella and basil 28
Roman-style gnocchi with pecorino Romano 44
potatoes: butter and bay leaf hasselback potatoes 124
carbonara potatoes 100
chicken legs with potatoes, lemons and capers 136

creamy fish pie with parsley, garlic and lemon gremolata 96

golden croquettes with mozzarella and ham 116

Mediterranean-style salmon with olives and cherry tomatoes 130

my healthy hangover brunch 120

my Nonna Assunta's pork ribs with potatoes and rosemary 115

potato cake 36

roast leg of lamb with rosemary, fennel and pepper 122

smashed potatoes with speck ham and Gorgonzola 110

prawns: creamy fish pie with parsley, garlic and lemon gremolata 96

panzanella salad with king prawns and ciabatta 63

prosecco, whole sea bream with lemon and 148

puff pastry: almond and raspberry frangipane tart 189

asparagus, Gorgonzola and honey tart 157

courgette and fontina tart 20

millefeuille with strawberries, Amaretto and pistachios 186

Mortadella, sour cherry, fontina and red onion sausage rolls 99

pizza puff sticks 72

pumpkin lasagne, roasted 119

R

ragù stile Bolognese 23

raspberries: almond and raspberry frangipane tart 189

rhubarb crumble with limoncello 178

rice: crispy arancine with ham and mozzarella 34

Milanese-style air fryer risotto 33

ricotta cheese: baked ricotta and courgettes with rosemary and pistachio nuts 58

cannelloni with spinach and ricotta 16

ricotta and panettone cheesecake with chocolate chips 184

ricotta e zucchine con rosmarino e pistacchi 58

risotto al forno stile Milanese 33

Roman-style gnocchi with pecorino Romano 44

Roman-style pizza with olives and semi-dried tomatoes 105

rotolino di salsiccia con mortadella e cipolle rosse 99

S

salads: fennel salad 148

panzanella salad with king prawns and ciabatta 63

slaw 144

salami: toasted 'raid the deli' picnic panino 69

salmon: Mediterranean-style salmon with olives and cherry tomatoes 130

salmone alla Mediterranea con olive e pomodorini 130

salsa tonnata 165

saltimbocca, chicken 52

saltimbocca alla Romana 52

sandwiches: toasted 'raid the deli' picnic panino 69

sausages: baked pasta with sausages, garlic, rosemary and mozzarella 84

Mortadella, sour cherry, fontina and red onion sausage rolls 99

sbriciolata con rabarbaro e limoncello 178

Scotch egg with Martini Bianco 93

sea bream with lemon and prosecco 148

Sicilian aubergines with red wine vinegar and green olives 18

slaw 144

spaghetti frittata with courgettes and pecorino Romano 133

speck: roasted pumpkin lasagne 119

smashed potatoes with speck ham and Gorgonzola 110

spicy glazed pork chops with hot honey and slaw 144

spiedini di agnello marinato con aglio, peperoni e cipolla rossa 138

spinach: cannelloni with spinach and ricotta 16

date-night steaks with Marsala and spinach 166

strawberries: millefeuille with strawberries, Amaretto and pistachios 186

succulent chicken burgers with rocket and Parmesan 90

succulent meatballs with spicy tomato sauce 31

super-crispy polenta chips with salsa tonnata 165

suprema di pollo con salsa di zafferano e limone 158

T

tagliata, topside 39

tagliata di manzo con rucola, scaglia di parmigiano e aceto balsamico 39

tarts: almond and raspberry frangipane tart 189

apricot jam tart with lemon zest 183

asparagus, Gorgonzola and honey tart 157

courgette and fontina tart with semi-dried tomatoes 20

toasted 'raid the deli' picnic panino 69

tomatoes: aubergine Parmigiana with spiced tomato and oozing mozzarella 40

Aunty Clara's stuffed aubergines with lentils and mozzarella 141

baked pasta with sausages, garlic, rosemary and mozzarella 84

Bolognese-style sauce 23

bruschetta with marinated tomatoes and creamy burrata 150

bucatini with aubergine, tomatoes and toasted almonds 134

cannelloni with spinach and ricotta 16

courgette and fontina tart with semi-dried tomatoes 20

gnocchi in pancetta, tomato and Parmesan sauce 108

gnocchi with tomato, mozzarella and basil 28

Mediterranean-style salmon with olives and cherry tomatoes 130

panzanella salad with king prawns and ciabatta 63

pizza chicken breasts 66

pizza puff sticks 72

Roman-style pizza with olives and semi-dried tomatoes 105

Sicilian aubergines with red wine vinegar and green olives 18

succulent meatballs with spicy tomato sauce 31

topside tagliata with rocket, Parmesan and balsamic 39

torta calda con panettone e vaniglia 177

torta con ricotta, panettone e cioccolato 184

torta di asparagi, gorgonzola e miele 157

torta di polenta, limoni e mandorle 194

torta salata con fontina e pomodorini semi-secchi 20

torta salata di pesce con gremolata 96

tortini caldi ripieni di cioccolato 196

tortini de Ferrero Rocher 180

tranci di polenta croccante con salsa tonnata 165

tuna: salsa tonnata 165

turkey breast, brandied 112

V

ventagli di patate al forno con burro e alloro 124

Z

zeppole di San Giuseppe 190–1

zucchine alla scapece 26

zucchine fritte 64

BLOOMSBURY PUBLISHING
Bloomsbury Publishing Plc
50 Bedford Square, London, WC1B 3DP, UK
29 Earlsfort Terrace, Dublin 2, Ireland

BLOOMSBURY, BLOOMSBURY PUBLISHING
and the Diana logo are trademarks of Bloomsbury Publishing Plc

First published in Great Britain in 2024
Text © Gino D'Acampo, 2024

Photographs © Haarala Hamilton, 2024

Gino D'Acampo and Haarala Hamilton have asserted their right under the Copyright, Designs and Patents Act,
1988, to be identified as Author and Photographer, respectively, of this work.

For legal purposes, the acknowledgements on page 198 constitute an extension of this copyright page.

A catalogue record for this book is available from the British Library.
ISBN: HB: 978-1-5266-8041-9; eBook: 978-1-5266-8503-2;
4 6 8 10 9 7 5 3

Project Editor: Lucy Bannell
Designer: Anna Green at Siulen Design
Photographer: Haarala Hamilton
Food Stylist: Katy McClelland
Assistant Food Stylist: Arnaud Berrabia
Prop Stylist: Jennifer Kay
Indexer: Vanessa Bird

Printed and bound in Germany by Mohn Media

MIX
Paper | Supporting
responsible forestry
FSC® C011124
FSC
www.fsc.org

To find out more about our authors and books,
visit www.bloomsbury.com and sign up for our newsletters.

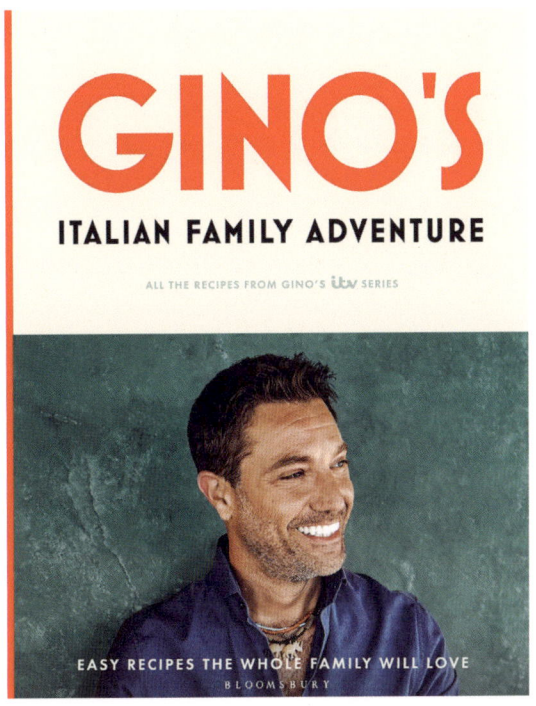